D0505997

THE AMERICAN LIBRARY

10, RUE DU GÉNÉRAL CAMOU
75007 PARIS

WITHDRAWN

The
Outsourcing
Handbook

The
Outsourcing
Handbook

How to Implement a Successful Outsourcing Process

Mark J Power
Kevin C Desouza
Carlo Bonifazi

RECOMMENDED BY
INSTITUTE OF DIRECTORS

KOGAN
PAGE

London and Philadelphia

This book has been endorsed by the Institute of Directors.

The endorsement is given to selected Kogan Page books which the IoD recognizes as being of specific interest to its members and providing them with up-to-date, informative and practical resources for creating business success. Kogan Page books endorsed by the IoD represent the most authoritative guidance available on a wide range of subjects including management, finance, marketing, training and HR.

The views expressed in this book are those of the authors and are not necessarily the same as those of the Institute of Directors.

Publisher's note

Every possible effort has been made to ensure that the information contained in this book is accurate at the time of going to press, and the publishers and authors cannot accept responsibility for any errors or omissions, however caused. No responsibility for loss or damage occasioned to any person acting, or refraining from action, as a result of the material in this publication can be accepted by the editor, the publisher or any of the authors.

First published in Great Britain and the United States in 2006 by Kogan Page Limited

Apart from any fair dealing for the purposes of research or private study, or criticism or review, as permitted under the Copyright, Designs and Patents Act 1988, this publication may only be reproduced, stored or transmitted, in any form or by any means, with the prior permission in writing of the publishers, or in the case of reprographic reproduction in accordance with the terms and licences issued by the CLA. Enquiries concerning reproduction outside these terms should be sent to the publishers at the undermentioned addresses:

120 Pentonville Road
London N1 9JN
United Kingdom
www.kogan-page.co.uk

525 South 4th Street, #241
Philadelphia PA 19147
USA

© Mark John Power, Kevin Clyde Desouza and Carlo Bonifazi, 2006

The right of Mark J Power, Kevin C Desouza and Carlo Bonifazi to be identified as the authors of this work has been asserted by them in accordance with the Copyright, Designs and Patents Act 1988.

ISBN 0 7494 4430 4

British Library Cataloguing-in-Publication Data

A CIP record for this book is available from the British Library.

Library of Congress Cataloging-in-Publication Data
Power, Mark John.
   The outsourcing handbook : how to implement a successful outsourcing process / Mark John Power, Kevin Clyde Desouza. Carlo Bonifazi.
     p. cm.
   Includes bibliographical references and index.
   ISBN 0-7494-4430-4
   1. Contracting out—Handbooks, manuals, etc. 2. Offshore outsourcing—Handbooks, manuals, etc. I. Desouza, Kevin C., 1979 – II. Bonifazi, Carlo. III. Title.
   HD2365.P69 2006
   658.4'058—dc22
                      2005031046

Typeset by Saxon Graphics Ltd, Derby
Printed and bound in Great Britain by Creative Print and Design (Wales), Ebbw Vale

658.405
P9710

Contents

Acknowledgements

All three of us would like to acknowledge the words of wisdom we continue to receive from Dr George Kraft. We are his former students and through the years Dr Kraft has continued to provide us with much needed counsel and encouragement. We can honestly say that Dr Kraft has given more to us than we can thank him for.

Mark – I would like to thank all the people who have been involved in the numerous outsourcing projects that I have had the pleasure to lead in the past 15 years. Specials thanks to my colleague and friend Manish Tomar for the many hours of collaboration through the years in pursuit of outsourcing excellence.

Kevin – I would like to acknowledge the support from the staff of the Engaged Enterprise and especially the researchers at the Institute for Engaged Business Research, the think-tank of the Engaged Enterprise. They tirelessly supported the book project by providing both administrative and research support. I am indebted to the many distinguished colleagues that I collaborate with on a daily basis. I would like to thank Clare Danes for her administrative and research support. As always, I am grateful to the support of my immediate and extended family – Mum, Dad, Kenneth, Karishma, uncles, aunts and the eclectic group of cousins.

Carlo – I would like to acknowledge the early pioneers of outsourcing that took those early journeys without a road map or a good set of instructions to follow, for their courage in proceeding head first into uncharted waters. Today's outsourcing practitioners don't need to be

quite that adventurous since they can benefit from a wealth of information available on lessons learnt that span the experiences of those
early pioneers to those of today.

We would like to thank our editor, Jon Finch at Kogan Page, for
recognizing the value of the work and providing us an opportunity to
get our ideas and thinking into print. A final word of thanks to you, our
readers, the management practitioners, for giving us your interest and
attention in the pages that follow.

Mark J Power
Kevin C Desouza
Carlo Bonifazi

About the authors

Mark J Power has 20 years of experience in the high-tech industry and has held senior management and executive positions in operations, strategic sourcing, supply management, contracts, information technology (IT) and research and development (R&D). He is a seasoned global outsourcing executive and a pioneer in the outsourcing education field. For the past 15 years, Mr Power has designed, implemented and managed multimillion-dollar manufacturing, IT and R&D outsourcing initiatives in the United States, Mexico, Europe, the Middle East and India.

Mr Power is the President of ROS Incorporated, an outsourcing education, process and consultancy company based in Chicago, Illinois. ROS Incorporated advises and educates organizations on outsourcing strategies, design and implementation by utilizing outsourcing best practices that maximize returns on outsourcing investments. Mr Power has a BA degree from Stonehill College, an MBA from Roosevelt University and an MS from Illinois Institute of Technology. He also holds CPM and APP certifications from the Institute of Supply Management and has been awarded six design patents in the area of call-center technology.

Kevin C Desouza is the President of the Engaged Enterprise, a strategy consulting firm with expertise in the areas of knowledge management, crisis management, strategic deployment of information systems and government and competitive intelligence assignments. He also serves as the Director of the Institute for Engaged Business

Research, a think-tank of the Engaged Enterprise. He has authored *Managing Knowledge with Artificial Intelligence* (Quorum Books, 2002), co-authored *Managing Information in Complex Organizations* (M E Sharpe, 2005) and *Engaged Knowledge Management* (Palgrave Macmillan, 2005) and edited *New Frontiers of Knowledge Management* (Palgrave Macmillan, 2005). In addition, he has published over 100 articles in prestigious practitioner and academic journals. Mr Desouza is frequently an invited speaker on a number of cutting-edge business and technology topics for national and international, industry and academic audiences.

Carlo Bonifazi has 25 years of diverse experience in the technology field and has held senior management positions in software development and production, product development, strategic alliances and IT. He has led global outsourcing product development and IT initiatives, including efforts in application development, network infrastructure, telecommunications, security, customer relationship management (CRM) systems and enterprise resource planning (ERP) systems.

Mr Bonifazi is the Co-founder and Vice President of ROS Incorporated, an outsourcing consultancy and training company based in Lisle, Illinois. ROS Incorporated advises and educates organizations on outsourcing strategies and the design and implementation of outsourcing best practices that maximize returns on outsourcing investments. Mr Bonifazi has a BS degree from the University of Illinois and an MS from Illinois Institute of Technology.

Preface

As a business practice, outsourcing is flourishing in almost every conceivable domain. Organizations today outsource software development, innovation and research and development efforts and even functional areas such as marketing, human resource administration and finance and accounting. Outsourcing of knowledge-intensive work is increasing at an astonishing rate. Just a few years ago, you would never have heard of companies outsourcing their research and development (R&D) areas; today, this is quite common. Moreover, outsourcing R&D even occurs when organizations realize that this is their core competency, ie the key differentiator between them and their competitors. The rationale is quite simple – an organization had better seek out and form alliances with companies that have mature processes in place, even in the areas of its core competencies, if it is to take advantage of the added value of mature practices.

One would hope that with the rise in outsourcing as a business phenomenon, managers and executives would be better equipped to handle the many challenges associated with outsourcing. Unfortunately, our experience tells us otherwise. We have seen a number of cases where organizations with good intentions and determined dedication fail miserably in their outsourcing efforts. What is even more interesting is that, over time, some of the failures seem to repeat themselves across organizations and even within the same organization. This realization led us to consider writing *The Outsourcing Handbook*. Our goal is to provide a hands-on and applied approach to exploring the intricacies of commencing, managing, renewing and/or terminating outsourcing engagements. We will focus on operational details of the outsourcing life cycle.

In writing this book we have made some deliberate decisions that need to be addressed up front. First, we have intentionally chosen not to focus on any specific category of outsourcing, for example outsourcing of software development or R&D. We believe that regardless of what is being outsourced, if managers execute the outsourcing process with rigor and clarity, success is almost guaranteed. In keeping with this intention, we feel the material presented here can be used by organizations of any size, and any orientation, ranging from the Fortune 100s to the small-to-medium sized enterprises (SMEs) and from those based in the United States or Europe to those in Asia and Australia. All organizations, regardless of size and location, must take a systemic approach to outsourcing if they hope to be successful. What varies from one organization to another are the variables of the processes themselves. By this we mean that a large organization might consider outsourcing a project worth US $100 million whereas the smaller foe may outsource a project worth US $5,000. Regardless of the amounts, as a proxy for the size of the project, both organizations must conduct steps of strategic assessment, needs analysis, vendor selection, etc with diligence and care to ensure success of their efforts. In the same vein, regardless of an organization being headquartered in London or Sydney or Mumbai, following good outsourcing methodology is a must. Here again, what will change based on the organization, and where it plans to outsource, are the variables of the process. For example, an organization in Mumbai that is planning to outsource work to China or the Philippines or even to the United States will have to account for different cultural issues from an organization in downtown Chicago that is planning to outsource work to rural Ziebach County, in South Dakota, United States. To sum up, the process we present in the pages that follow is intended to be general and somewhat broad. Readers can follow and implement the outlined process, with ease, by incorporating the details of their organization and environments.

Second, we do understand that outsourcing the manufacturing of widgets is quite different from sourcing of knowledge-intensive tasks. Recognizing this, we focus on the latter. Knowledge-intensive work, to our minds, involves tasks that call for specialized expertise possessed by different parties. This differs from traditional manufacturing outsourcing in one important aspect. In a manufacturing assignment, knowledge about the production process such as design specifications, assembly methods and quality metrics are transferred from the organization to the outsourcing vendor. For example, in the case of production manufacturing, Nike hands over design specifications and other details to its manufacturing plants that are responsible for adhering to these specifications and delivering the products; knowledge flows one way. In knowledge-intensive sourcing, there is a dyadic flow of knowledge. Both parties, the client and the vendor, are experts in their domains. The client passes on business knowledge to the vendor, who must then apply its own expertise in the context of the client's business knowledge to deliver the products and/or services. It is this two-way flow of knowledge and information between the client and the vendor that makes knowledge-intensive sourcing more interesting and consequently more challenging to manage.

The third and final decision was to write this book in a simple and conversational style and avoid jargon as much as possible. We believe that management of outsourcing efforts should be easy – it should not be rocket science! You need not possess a PhD in business management to be successful in outsourcing. Each chapter in this book is written in an easily accessible and process-oriented format. We provide you with tools that you can take to your organization and implement for increased success with sourcing efforts.

A few comments on what this book will *not* cover are also required. We will not propose any grand theories or offer academically acquired knowledge here. Instead, we will share with you lessons we have learnt from being in the outsourcing trenches from the three broad perspectives of the authors. The strength of the book you are about to read is the blend of these three different sets of experiences and perspectives to give you a cogent and comprehensive understanding of outsourcing management issues. It is our firm belief that all three perspectives must be appreciated to be successful at leveraging outsourcing as a strategic weapon.

It has been our pleasure to put this book together and we hope you enjoy it. One of the joys of writing a book is the comments one receives from one's readers. While we have done our best to envision what material would be of interest to you, we are sure we may have understressed an important point or overemphasized a simple concept. We invite you to share your comments with us on the material worth of the book; please contact us with any issues, comments, questions, critiques or even praise! If we can be of any assistance to your organization as you chart your outsourcing trajectory, remember that we are only an e-mail away. Happy reading!

Mark J Power (mpower@rosourcing.com)
Kevin C Desouza (kev.desouza@gmail.com)
Carlo Bonifazi (cbonifazi@rosourcing.com)

Introduction

Outsourcing is made up of two words – 'out' and 'sourcing'. Hence, to define outsourcing we must first be clear on the meaning of 'sourcing'. Sourcing refers to the act of transferring work, responsibilities and decision rights to someone else. As managers, we constantly delegate or source work to our employees. Why do we engage in outsourcing? We must source out work because there are others who can do it cheaper, faster, better and because we have other, more important, demands on our resources. It will be futile for a manager to expel efforts booking a business trip, as it involves intricacies such as finding flights, booking hotel rooms, reserving a rental car, that, need not be remunerated at the manager's salary. Every minute a manager spends on this administrative task is a minute taken away from doing his or her real work. The organization will run at a loss by having a manager conduct the administrative task rather than sourcing it to an individual who is costing the organization less in terms of salary. Hence costs, both real (the salary) and opportunity (the time, attention and effort), are important determinants in the sourcing decision.

Besides efficiency, outsourcing also helps get work done more effectively. For instance, compared to most managers a financial trader has superior knowledge about the working of the markets and the issues of stock pricing and appreciation. Hence, we employ brokers and financial planners to manage our portfolios. Even if we could make stock purchases and sales efficiently, for instance via the internet as is possible today, we would still lack the required expertise and knowledge to make good decisions. Hence, outsourcing of the task to an expert provides access to the expertise, which can be used to further our goals.

Similar dynamics occur at the organizational level. No organization is self-sufficient, nor does any organization have unlimited resources. However, in most organizations there are unlimited wants. These wants compete for the scarce resources of the organization. Organizations must source work that can be conducted by others at lower cost and with greater effectiveness or it will waste valuable resources in the pursuit of capabilities that can be readily purchased from others. This pursuit results in poor management since, by its very nature, management is the work of achieving objectives in an effective manner utilizing the least amount of resources. Moreover, engaging in outsourcing allows an organization access to expertise, knowledge and capabilities found outside its bounds.

Sourcing is normally conducted with an external party – ie external to the unit conducting the sourcing, hence the word 'out'. A group within the organization can outsource some work to another group. Similarly, an organization can outsource work to another organization or person who is external to it.

Outsourcing initiatives have evolved from short-term projects focused on cost savings to executive-level business strategies that enable companies to gain – and sustain – revenues and profits in the competitive global marketplace. There are two outcomes of the surge of interest in outsourcing:

- Outsourcing has been bantered around as the next big revolution – the new management buzzword.
- When people talk about outsourcing they are normally not talking about the same 'outsourcing'.

To address these two issues, the focus of this chapter will be to introduce the concept of outsourcing, as we see it. We will begin by defining outsourcing and outlining the three major players in the outsourcing relationship – the client, the vendor and the work. We will then discuss the various factors that have made outsourcing a prominent business strategy. Next, we will discuss the various types of outsourcing project organizations can get involved in. An appreciation for the various types of outsourcing will result in better communication about outsourcing endeavors. We then enumerate the skills executives need to possess in order to be successful at managing outsourcing efforts. We conclude the chapter with a road map for the rest of this book.

What is outsourcing?

Sourcing, as discussed above, is the act of transferring work from one entity to another. Outsourcing is the act of transferring the work to an external party. Whether or not to outsource is the decision of whether to make or buy. Organizations are continuously faced with the decision of whether to expend resources to create an asset, resource, product or service internally or to buy it from an external party. If the organization chooses to buy, it is engaging in outsourcing. An outsourcing initiative calls for the transfer of factors of production, the resources used to perform the work and the decision rights, or responsibilities for making decisions. The organization transferring these is referred to as the client, the organization that conducts the work and makes decisions is the vendor, and the scope of the work is captured in a project (see Figure 0.1).

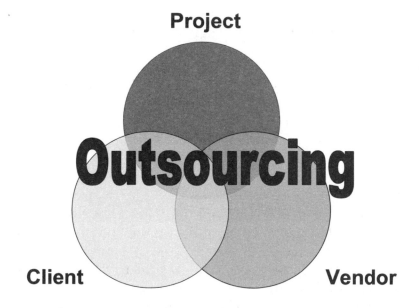

Figure 0.1 Components of outsourcing

The client

A client is the person or organization that would like to outsource a given project. Normally, this entity is thinking about utilizing outsourcing as a strategic tool. We are writing this book from the client perspective. Our goal is to help an organization that wants to conduct outsourcing do it effectively and efficiently.

Clients can range in scope and size. A client can be an entire organization or a unit within an organization. If the project being outsourced is the entire IT department of the organization, we can say that the organization is the client. However, if we are only outsourcing the payroll functionality of the human resource department, the client is the human resource department, though indirectly the entire organization is also the client.

The vendor

The vendor is the service provider who will take over and conduct the outsourced work. Vendors come in many shapes and sizes. For instance, a vendor can be an external organization, which is most often the case. However, a vendor can also be a subsidiary of the organization. For instance, Dell Computers has opened operations in places like Brazil, where they own the outfits. Dell routinely sends software work to these locations because of the availability of a skilled workforce and cost savings. Hence, Dell is engaging in what might be called 'wholly-owned outsourcing' by outsourcing work to subsidiaries that it owns, where it can get the work done for a much lower price but with the same quality.

Vendors can be differentiated based on where they are located. Some vendors are located onshore or in the same area as the client. Others are located near-shore, as in the case of potential Canadian companies for US clients. Finally, vendors can be offshore, as in the case of Indian companies for British clients.

The project

The third component is the actual work being outsourced. In the past, the most common form of such work was manufacturing or labor-intensive projects. Today, however, there is a move towards the outsourcing of more complex forms of work, such as software development or R&D. These projects differ from the old manufacturing projects in several ways.

First, they are more loosely defined than manufacturing projects. Putting together a software project involves much more creativity than running a basic assembly line to make a piece of clothing for which there are pre-specified guidelines.

Second, since the work involves more knowledge-intensive tasks, it requires the use of a more skilled labor force. Third, most projects today are more complex owing to the way communications are handled using IT, the cross-functional nature of project teams and the presence of multiple stakeholders, many of who may be in different locations and may work for different organizations. Outsourcing projects also involves one more important feature – collaborations between organizations that do not necessarily share the same interest or goals. The client organization will normally want to get the work done at the most superior quality for the lowest possible price. The vendor wants to maximize its revenues from the project. These differences in objectives, if not managed appropriately during the contracting and negotiating phases of the outsourcing life cycle, will result in a disastrous business relationship.

Factors driving the need to outsource

Outsourcing has moved from initiatives that were financially motivated to the current stage of being strategically motivated. Financially motivated outsourcing efforts have been around since the early days of commerce. Manufacturing work, such as garment production, has long been outsourced to locations in South East Asia. The goal of these efforts was to get the best financial deal in terms of lowest cost of production. These efforts were mainly one-sided; information and requirements moved from the client to the vendor, who would then construct the product and/or service and deliver this back to the client. Information and knowledge would seldom flow back from the vendor to the client, as the client was assumed to be more knowledgeable than the vendor. In financially driven outsourcing efforts, it was common for a firm to structure a long-term deal with a single vendor so as to get the best possible discounts and secure the most stable relationship. After all, the goal here was to offload work to places where it could be done at lower cost.

Strategically driven outsourcing efforts are capability- and competency-intensive. The focus here is to tap into specialized expertise, knowledge, processes and capabilities found outside the organization, and to use these as inputs to help improve the effectiveness and efficiency of operations. More important, if done properly, strategically driven outsourcing efforts can not only help operations, but can also contribute to the strategic and competitive advantages of the organization.

Strategic outsourcing often involves partnerships between the client organization and multiple vendors. As a prime example consider the case of Dell Computers. Dell does not hold large amounts of computer hardware in its inventory; instead its core competency is its information systems and supply chain management systems. Dell takes in customer orders, and then coordinates the fulfillment process. To be successful in this, Dell must rely on a vast network of suppliers and manufacturers, not only for the products, but also for knowledge. Dell realizes that it does not have the necessary resources to have up-to-date information about each and every component of computer hardware. Such knowledge resides in the minds of Dell's business partners and hence Dell must not only send order information to these suppliers, but must also access the knowledge possessed by them. In addition, Dell must ensure that knowledge from one supplier is shared with the others, so that each one benefits from improved knowledge and insights. Strategically driven outsourcing efforts involve such collaboration between the client and multiple vendors, because the client organization is focused on getting the best breed of knowledge and expertise, as these have serious ramifications on its strategic and competitive advantages.

There are several factors that are influencing firms to consider outsourcing as a business strategy (see Figure 0.2). We will now enumerate these, recognizing the fact that some firms may be influenced more by some of these factors than others.

Access to resources and knowledge is important, not ownership

The earlier thinking about the ownership of factors of production for securing competitive advantages is outdated. Today, the more important detail is how an organization can access external resources and knowledge, rather than trying to own the resources. No organization is

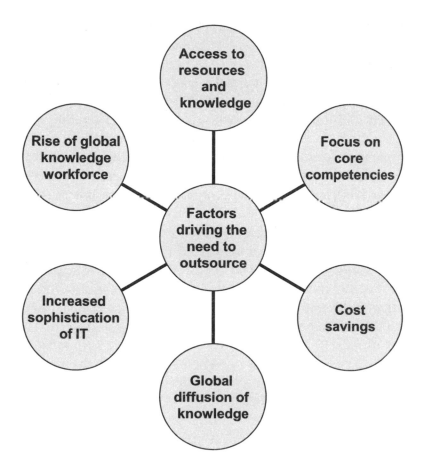

Figure 0.2 Factors driving the need to outsource

self-sufficient. Being self-sufficient is not economically viable for a basic reason – opportunity cost, which is the value derived from the best alternative use of a resource. If organizations try to do everything and spend all their resources to create expertise, skills and technology, they are under-utilizing their resources. Other firms in the marketplace may be able to provide them access to necessary resources at lower cost than it would take them to produce these resources.

Moreover, sometimes the resources provided by external parties may be of far superior quality than organizations can produce internally. There are many cases of outsourcing agreements where relationships are forged not just for basic cost saving but to get access to needed expertise, skills and technology. For example, Aon Corporation has outsourced the management of its US data centers, telecommunications networks, desktop support and help-desk services to Computer Sciences Corporation (CSC) (McDougall, 2004a, 2004b). In addition to the cost saving, the main benefits of the outsourcing agreement would include access to the state of the art in security practices and techniques – the core competencies of CSC – to help the organization better plan for business continuity and security management. In another case, in 2004 the British Broadcasting Corporation (BBC) crafted an outsourcing relationship of US $3.7 billion with Siemens Business Services Ltd to take over its technology sector. As part of the deal, the BBC will sell its wholly-owned commercial subsidiary, BBC Technology Holdings Ltd, to Siemens. Siemens will provide the BBC with necessary expertise and innovative solutions to help it realize its goal of being a leader in desktop news content delivery. The bottom line is that innovative knowledge is required in almost all areas of operations for a business, but the cost of creating this knowledge is significant. Hence, rather than expending resources to create such knowledge, organizations are purchasing this knowledge from external sources.

Cost savings

The predominant reason given for engaging in outsourcing is the cost savings, which are realized in several ways. First, cost savings can come from the simple move from fixed to variable cost models. In the fixed-cost model, you own all the resources and have to pay for their acquisition, upkeep and maintenance. These costs are fixed and occur no matter if you use the resource or not. For example, if you own a car you have certain fixed costs regardless of how much you drive it, such as maintenance or parking. If you drive the vehicle, then your expenses, such as fuel, increase. Under the variable-cost model, you do not incur the fixed costs associated with maintaining the asset but only pay a fee when you use the assets or access them, such as when renting a car. You are bound to save some costs when moving from fixed to variable cost, especially when the resources you use are not needed on a regular basis.

Second, cost savings can come from the company doing the outsourced work. In the case of software development, most of the current outsourcing is occurring with companies in the so-called developing world. Here the wages and costs of labor are quite low compared to those in Western Europe or the United States. The savings in salaries can be significant, as in most IT projects labor costs comprise the greatest proportion of the costs.

Third, other cost savings could result from beneficial tax treaties and other foreign-trade agreements, wherein governments may encourage multinational and international corporations to open up businesses in the developing countries by giving tax concessions and other setup benefits.

Focus on core competencies

Outsourcing not only involves the transfer of work, but also the transfer of decision rights. By transferring decision rights, the organization is reducing its need to focus high levels of resources on the effort of decision making. The vendor takes on the responsibility for decision making and is held accountable for the decision outcomes about achieving project goals. Transferring decision rights and accountability allows the client to pay more attention to its core competencies. Without engaging in outsourcing, the organization will perhaps not focus on areas in which it should invest manager attention and efforts.

Every organization has its core competencies; some have better developed and mature ones and this is what makes them industry leaders. When engaging in outsourcing, it is absolutely essential that a client organization is able to tap into the core competency of the vendor, not just for the simple task of sourcing the work, but also for knowledge. Knowledge from the vendor, especially in the area of the core competency, can help the client re-architect, redesign and re-engineer its business processes so as to be better suited to achieve greater competitive advantages. This has been the critical shift in focus over recent years, as outsourcing efforts become more mature. Clients are no longer looking only for cost economies, but also for a business partner who can contribute to the strategic efforts of the company by providing it with expertise and competencies that are not found in-house.

An outcome of being able to focus on core competencies is that it allows the organization to rethink its organization structure and restructure or realign itself. Think about narrowing down your long to-do list and prioritizing it by items that are urgent and central and those that are peripheral. Doing this will help clean up your view of what needs to be done immediately, and what can wait. Organizations are too often busy *doing* things and sometimes they do so at the expense of stopping to think about whether what is being done is indeed the most important or beneficial for the future of the organization. This results in lack of clear goal attainment and success. Organizations may be conducting work in projects that do not contribute to their core mission, or are in conflict with other projects. They may also be spending inordinate resources on tasks that are considered auxiliary, rather than core. Getting focused on what really matters, ie the core competencies, and outsourcing the rest, helps the organization better manage its activities. In some cases, as we will discuss in Chapter 3 on strategic assessment, an organization may have too many core competencies to focus on, and may even decide to outsource a handful of them to external vendors who may be able to do the work at lower cost and/or better.

Factors driving global outsourcing efforts

The business practice of offshoring focuses on the relocation of labor-intensive service industry functions to locations remote to the business center, such as India, Ireland or the Philippines. Two main changes in the business environment have enabled offshoring. First, the improvement in international telecommunications capacity, and the associated reduction in global telecommunications costs, is fundamental to the economics of offshoring. Second and just as important, over the past two decades the PC has enabled the computerization and digitization of most business services. As a result of these two changes, information can now be transmitted over long distances at very low cost and with little or no loss of quality. These changes make organizational boundaries and national borders much less important in deciding the location of service functions.

As a simple example, consider the task of payroll processing today as compared with a decade ago. In the past, companies seldom outsourced payroll processing, for most it was an in-house activity. Ceridian and other payroll processing organizations began to emerge in the late 1990s and started to lure such work away from companies. Companies found cost advantages in moving the processing of pay slips to such organizations. Soon after, developments in use of the internet enabled the creation of employee portals that could be used by employees to handle much of their remuneration and benefits management. Paperwork was being reduced in favor of digitization. As the sophistication of telecommunication infrastructures and security protocols of information transmission improved, payroll work started its move overseas. Today, it is not an aberration to see companies whose payroll is managed by an office in India or the Philippines, though their outsourcing vendor may have its headquarters in the United States or the UK.

Factors that are really enabling global outsourcing include growing pools of a highly skilled, educated workforce, available, for example, beyond the US market. Candidates have PhDs and Masters degrees in computer science and in computer engineering, and are well experienced in this area. Another consideration is the state-of-the-art facilities and infrastructure that are available out there in the global marketplace. Some of the infrastructure and facilities across India and China are much better than those, for example, currently within the United States.

Another factor that has contributed to the increase in global outsourcing is the sophistication of collaborative technology solutions. Today, we have a wide array of devices that can be used to communicate with our counterparts across the globe. Mobile phones, e-mail, video conferencing, web conferencing and instant messaging are a few of the gamut of collaborative tools available. The costs of such tools have decreased sizably over the years. In some cases, they are even available for free. Microsoft, AOL and other companies offer customers use of their Instant Messaging software, which can be used for text, voice and even image and document sharing, for free.

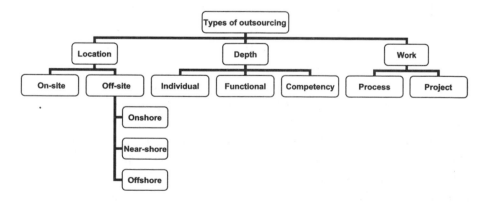

Figure 0.3 Types of outsourcing

Types of outsourcing

There is a wide assortment of outsourcing categories and models, each with its own strengths and weaknesses, and management concerns (see Figure 0.3). Outsourcing efforts can be segmented by location, ie where the work is done: on-site or off-site. On-site work involves having members of the vendor's team conduct work within the premises of the client organization. Off-site work is where the vendor conducts work at its location.

Within off-site work arrangements work can be onshore, near-shore and offshore. Onshore is where a vendor conducts work within the same country as the client. In some of the rural areas of the United States, especially around settlements and reservations of American Indian tribes, in places like South Dakota, North Dakota and parts of Utah, we have been seeing the emergence of consulting firms that are attractive vendors for onshore outsourcing of IT work (Field, 2001a, 2001b). These organizations can price their services somewhere in between what is charged to do the work in the major cities in the United States and the prices charged by offshore vendors. The cost of living for employees is low and there is availability of skilled labor to draw on. One of the clear benefits of outsourcing to an onshore location is the fact that there are fewer cultural issues to contend with. Language issues and work disruptions owing to significant time differences are minimized. The use of onshore vendors is particularly attractive when the work being outsourced is of a sensitive nature, such as work dealing with medical or financial information where there are regulations in place that prevent it being sent to offshore vendors owing to security and privacy risks.

Near-shore arrangements in the United States involve moving work outside the country to neighboring locations. For example, a lot of US companies have begun to use Canadian companies as viable business partners in call centers and software development projects. Similarly, West European countries have begun to explore the talent pool in Russia and some of the emerging East European nations for outsourcing work. Besides the cost advantage of doing work in the near-shore location, there are other advantages including no major cultural differences, cheaper travel and communication costs (it is a lot cheaper to fly to Canada from the United States than it is to fly to

India), and no major time zone differences, which prevents disruption of work and eases work patterns.

Finally, there are offshore arrangements where work is sent to countries that are at a considerable distance from the client. For example, India has become the dominant country for the outsourcing of software work. Organizations in the United States, the UK, Canada and Australia, among other countries, have outsourcing projects with Indian companies. As discussed earlier there are several key factors that make offshoring of work an attractive proposition.

Outsourcing projects can also be segmented by their depth level: individual, functional or competency. Individual outsourcing involves outsourcing specific positions out of the organization. Examples include the outsourcing of positions such as competitive intelligence analyst, web designer or public relations personnel. This is the simplest form of outsourcing, as the organization is engaging in the hiring of a single staff function, much like hiring a full-time consultant. Organizations engage in individual outsourcing when they need expertise in a niche area and for a specific time period. For instance, consider the case of a web designer. The chances are that the organization is not going to make major overhauls to its website on a daily basis. The organization, however, would like to keep its website current by adding new items such as current news and happenings. To handle this task, a full-time web designer working the stipulated 40 hours a week is not required. The organization is best served by outsourcing this function to a person who can be paid on an hourly basis and be called upon as needed to make updates to the website.

Functional outsourcing involves the outsourcing of an individual functional area, also known as a cost center. Outsourcing of accounts payable, purchasing, receiving and payroll are all examples of functional outsourcing. Functional outsourcing can be considered an amalgamation or higher-order version of individual outsourcing. Here, the organization has decided to outsource an entire domain of work, most commonly motivated by cost savings and superior expertise possessed by vendors. The third parties are able to deliver the service at low cost because of economies of scale, and it is in their best interest to keep updated with new tax and human resource laws in order to function effectively.

Competency outsourcing involves outsourcing of activities that control how products and/or services flow through the organization.

Examples include inbound logistics, technology development and human resource management. Competency outsourcing is the higher-order construct to functional outsourcing, as it involves the outsourcing of multiple functions. Here, the organization must have a great deal of trust and confidence in the vendor organization's ability to deliver on the project, as there will be serious negative impacts if work stoppage or other delivery issues arise.

Outsourcing efforts can also be classified by examining the nature of work – whether it is process-oriented or project-oriented work. Process-oriented work usually involves the outsourcing of a well-structured, standardized and documented process, for example, outsourcing of a payroll function. Project-oriented work, on the other hand, involves the outsourcing of unique and non-routine, unstructured and non-standardized work, for example software development. Process-oriented outsourcing is easier to manage as it involves a structured process and one that organizations understand fairly well, thereby making it easier to manage. Project-oriented work is most often more laborious to manage as organizations do not quite understand all the intricacies of the work and there is greater risk in handling work where managers have neither the necessary information nor deep experience.

Skills needed to manage outsourcing efforts

In order to be successful at leading outsourcing efforts, you must develop certain competencies. This book will help get you started in several areas, but should not be viewed as the end; rather, as a means to the end. Of the many skills that you may possess, here are a few that you may want to sharpen or start oiling.

Good decision making in high uncertainty environments is a critical skill when managing outsourcing efforts. While outsourcing initiatives are not entirely novel to organizations, their complexity, risk and impact on organizations has never been higher. A consequent factor of this is the need to make decisions in uncertain environments. You must be able to make decisions with incomplete information, have the foresight to plan ahead using scenarios, think through various alternatives, and – most importantly – find ways to reduce the uncertainty associated with making decisions. Following a process-driven and structured approach to outsourcing will help this effort, by providing you with a set of tools and techniques that can be used to journey through the uncharted outsourcing waters. Through experiences with outsourcing, you will learn how to ask the right questions, seek out the right information and synthesize information in a time-sensitive manner in order to make swift decisions.

Marketing and positioning skills are also vital. Outsourcing efforts require an organization to embrace change. Most of the time, this change is not pleasant to communicate to employees, as they have to give up their comfort zones of operations and begin operating under new premises. In some cases, they may not even have a job when the changes include rightsizing (or downsizing). Hence, it is very important to have good marketing and selling skills. You must be able to convince your audience about your idea, and more importantly, rally support behind it. This is especially vital when seeking senior management support. Without adequate marketing skills, it will be difficult to position the outsourcing strategy as a win-win situation. If this does not happen, rest assured that your outsourcing efforts will be in vain, as it takes dedicated effort on the part of a large number of individuals to make outsourcing a success, and they must first be convinced that the idea genuinely merits their dedicated work.

Negotiating and relationship-building skills are essential for building a good outsourcing relationship with your vendors. Much like what is said about genius, outsourcing efforts are 5 per cent inspiration and 95 per cent perspiration. Much of the perspiration comes from engaging in long and sometimes grueling meetings with vendors, where details of the outsourcing project are ironed out and the contracts are specified. Once the outsourcing project is under way, you need to expel efforts to ensure that what was agreed upon is actually occurring. To do this successfully, it is important that you have excellent negotiating skills and can manage the relationship so as to attain the organizational objectives with minimal hostilities with the vendor. Negotiating skills are more critical when engaging with vendors who are in different countries, since you must be sensitive to cultural issues. Failure to appreciate and manage the subtleties in cultures can transform well-meant actions into insensitive and rude gestures.

Finally, it is important to have knowledge-management skills. In our experience, there is one factor that challenges most executives in outsourcing efforts – dealing with multiple sources of data, information and knowledge. On any matter regarding outsourcing, you are bound to have more perspectives than you care for. Some of these perspectives come from speaking to your staff, others come from external sources such as vendors, reading business magazines, talking to peers, listening to academics and even surfing the internet. The end result is information overload. You become paralyzed by the barrage of information and cannot execute a coherent strategy. It is important to possess a vast breadth of knowledge about the organization and its industry, to be able to articulate clearly the organization's mission, its value statements, core competencies, key stakeholders and their interests and its future expansion plans. Then, you need to have a team of experts who have the necessary deep knowledge in the domains and must rely on their counsel to manage the outsourcing effort. You must be able to manage conflicts in information from different sources, and also be able to triangulate incoming information, so as to ensure that the information being acted on is the most reliable, complete and credible at any point.

In the final analysis, an executive tasked with managing outsourcing efforts must be able to put all skills and expertise into turbo boost or overdrive. Unfortunately, there are no colleges or degrees that can certify an executive as an 'outsourcing manager'. Most executives assume this role after a background in a given domain, whether it is finance, management, information systems, procurement, etc. Outsourcing cuts through multiple functional areas, so the onus of breaking through silo-based thinking lies with the executive. This thinking may have worked when overseeing a functional domain, but to manage an outsourcing effort, an executive needs to grasp the big picture of the entire organization.

Road map for the book

In the next chapter, we will discuss the common traps organizations fall prey to when conducting outsourcing efforts. We enumerate these up front, so that you will be able to pay close attention to the successive chapters that discuss how these errors can be avoided by following a rigorous process. Chapter 2 will introduce the outsourcing life cycle, then Chapters 3–10 explore each stage of the life cycle in depth. We conclude with Chapter 11, where we describe best practices found in organizations that have been successful in using outsourcing as a strategic weapon and outline what the future might hold for outsourcing.

1 Ten common traps of outsourcing

As discussed in the Introduction, employing outsourcing as a strategy can offer organizations a number of interesting and quite enticing benefits. In our experience, seldom do most companies realize all that outsourcing has to offer. In many organizations, outsourcing strategies are often considered the silver bullet to resolve problems. Outsourcing has been touted as the ideal way for organizations to reduce costs, focus on core business processes, improve services, enhance skills, reduce time to market and increase overall competitive advantage. Although many of these attributes accrue to a well-planned, soundly implemented and capably managed outsourcing initiative, many organizations are naive about the commitment and discipline it takes to reap these benefits. Organizations fail to realize the impact outsourcing will have on their people, processes, methods and tools. This naive attitude results in outsourcing engagements that are too often disastrous rather than fruitful experiences. In the end, organizations may try to move their failed outsourcing initiative to another vendor and repeat the same mistakes or engage in 'back sourcing', ie bringing the outsourced work back in-house and expending internal resources to complete the work.

In order to ground the rest of the material in this book in some context, we think it is necessary to state the common errors made when outsourcing. Recognition of these errors will help you recognize, evaluate and address them at various stages of the outsourcing life cycle.

Ten common traps of outsourcing

1. Lack of management commitment
2. Minimal knowledge of outsourcing methodologies
3. Lack of an outsourcing communications plan
4. Failure to recognize outsourcing business risks
5. Failure to tap into external sources of knowledge
6. Not dedicating the best and brightest internal resources
7. Rushing through the initiative
8. Not appreciating cultural differences
9. Minimizing what it will take to make the vendor productive
10. Poor relationship management programs

Based on Power, Bonifazi and Desouza (2004)

The ten common traps

1. Lack of management commitment

Executives mistakenly believe that outsourcing is a quick fix for core problems plaguing their businesses, from bloated cost structures, substandard quality, insufficient internal skills and extended product development life cycles to a lack of business focus. This thinking is the first trap that ensnares the client organization in a disastrous outsourcing relationship.

When management attempts to lead outsourcing initiatives without understanding the long-term ramifications to their organization's overall business strategy, they cannot articulate an execution strategy that can be driven down to all levels of the organization. This results in ambiguous contracts, milestones and deliverables, and creates conflicts between their organization and their vendor. As companies race to outsource larger pieces of their business, a majority of executives minimize the scope, time, cost and resources required to formulate successful outsourcing strategies. These deficiencies are magnified in the execution stages of the outsourcing initiative and usually result in unfulfilled expectations.

True commitment to a successful outsourcing initiative requires executive involvement and perseverance to resolve fundamental business problems prior to establishing an outsourcing initiative and passing the problems on to a potential vendor. Executives need to lead the charge, assess the business and ask some difficult questions:

- Are we competitive in our marketplace, both locally and globally?
- Do we know what our core competencies are?
- Can our customers, suppliers and competitors validate our core competencies?
- Do we really know our cost structure?
- Do we have the right strategies, management, people and processes to stay competitive?
- Can outsourcing be a core piece of the business strategy that attains desired organizational results?
- Do we have the pertinent information to identify potential areas that may be candidates for outsourcing?

These questions must be asked and answered by the executive team or the initiative will have a high probability of failure and will be tossed away like so many 'flavor of the month' management initiatives. Chapter 3 discusses the intricacies of conducting a strategic assessment of the organization. One critical part of conducting this assessment is to get involvement and support for the outsourcing efforts from senior management.

2. Minimal knowledge of outsourcing methodologies

Many organizations get caught up in the hype of the outsourcing craze and forget that it is a complex business strategy. To be successful, organizations must identify, establish and implement proven method-ologies and industry best practices. Most organizations fail to admit and recognize that their knowledge of the outsourcing life cycle and management discipline is minimal.

How many organizations really have people, processes, procedures and tools that can guide the organization through the outsourcing life cycle, including strategy formulation, requests for proposal, vendor identification and selection, contract negotiation, project transition and outsourcing relationship management? The majority of organizations operate in a haphazard fashion, hoping that things will turn out as planned. In our experience, there are only a handful of organizations with dedicated teams and centers that oversee outsourcing efforts.

Mature organizations serious about making their outsourcing initiative successful seek out industry best practices and benchmark successful outsourcing initiatives. They invest in training their personnel on proven methodologies and codify them relative to their internal processes, while collecting and analyzing metrics data to measure their progress. These organizations believe that outsourcing is a core competency and critical to their global business competitiveness.

3. Lack of an outsourcing communications plan

Outsourcing represents a paradigm shift in the way businesses operate as they look to reduce fixed costs and move costs to a variable model, built up and broken down on a project-by-project basis. Outsourcing rumors can impact all levels of the organization, instilling fear and apprehension and creating a negative impact on organizational productivity. For instance, in many organizations, long before the start of an outsourcing initiative employee productivity decreases, lower turnover and low employee morale become pervasive and lack of trust in the organization leads to poor service and product deliveries.

Companies that have product portfolios based on homegrown proprietary technologies requiring high levels of customer domain knowledge are very vulnerable during outsourcing initiatives. In these organizations, a huge amount of intellectual capital typically resides in small pockets of experts who must be identified. Communication with these employees is essential to ensure that they understand their roles and are properly compensated to stay through the outsourcing initiative. Companies that fail to do this are at risk of seeing key employees and intellectual capital leave the organization during the outsourcing initiative, crippling their chances for success.

A formal communication plan that articulates the purpose of the outsourcing initiative including key milestones should describe the organizational processes that are involved, including time lines and descriptions of how communications will flow throughout the organization. Organizations must be straightforward with their employees on the long-term impacts of outsourcing. These may include new job assignments, current employees being transferred to the outsourcing vendor and possible job elimination. It is important to address all questions and issues that may arise from the employee community in a timely manner, realizing that there will not always be support from employees. In these communications, it is important to focus on the business impacts of the outsourcing initiative and be careful not to single out units or processes that may have been problematic to the organization in the past. Organizations should always 'take the high road' and treat all impacted personnel professionally and with the utmost respect.

As an organization passes through the stages of the outsourcing life cycle, it is important to communicate status to the stakeholders. For instance, after completion of the strategic assessment (see Chapter 3), the organization should communicate the findings, such as the areas that are candidates for outsourcing. Upon completion of the needs analysis (discussed in Chapter 4), the organization must communicate findings, such as the details of the outsourcing plan that should include answers to questions such as:

- What is going to be outsourced?
- When is it to be outsourced?
- Who will be impacted?
- What plans are in place to mitigate the impact on those affected?

4. Failure to recognize outsourcing business risks

Outsourcing is a risky proposition and, in some cases, a leap of faith as organizations move people, functions, applications and processes to external vendors in the hope of improving overall competitiveness. Crucial questions to consider are:

- What happens if the vendor fails to meet your business objective?
- What does it mean to the business?
- What are the alternatives?

Besides the obvious risk of the outsourcing work not being conducted or falling below expectations, a key issue on the minds of executives today is the protection of intellectual property, including confidential business data, trade secrets, copyrights, trademarks and patents. The physical security and protection of intellectual property are critical issues, particularly since countries have differing legal systems. Ask yourself these questions:

- Do vendor candidates have a proven track record of maintaining strong security protocol at their locations?
- Do they have procedures to protect intellectual property?

The best method for ensuring the protection of intellectual property is to limit outsourcing to locations that can guarantee impeccable security. Although there is no sure way to eliminate risk, there are many ways to reduce it by following a disciplined outsourcing life cycle methodology. Among the questions to ask are:

- Is the outsourcing strategy realistic and executable?
- Have you identified and documented your intellectual property?
- Are the schedules realistic?
- Has the vendor been properly screened?
- Does the contract reflect the mutual interests of both client and vendor?
- Are there shared risks and rewards?
- Are there clear objective metrics and deliverables?
- Is there a documented relationship management plan?

Veteran organizations begin their outsourcing relationships by addressing what happens when the relationship ends. Doing this places risk-reduction strategies in the forefront and eliminates surprises in the client and vendor organizations. Business is all about managing risks, and outsourcing is no exception. One of the business areas that must be carefully assessed for risk is computer/network security. Companies must be realistic about their internal security capabilities. Organizations that specialize in this field probably do a much better job of security on an ongoing basis, a phenomenon that will increase as companies reduce staff and training expenses. Organizations must carefully examine and mitigate risk, as a single significant episode has the potential to shut down the business.

Chapter 3 will discuss how to conduct a risk assessment at the strategic level, while Chapter 5 will elaborate on how to evaluate the outsourcing vendor in order to minimize possible risks. Chapter 9 will discuss the details of creating exit strategies and backup plans to counter possible outsourcing risks.

5. Failure to tap into external sources of knowledge

Most organizations fail to recognize the complexities and business ramifications of their outsourcing decisions. Consequently, they rely exclusively on internal resources to guide the organization through the initiative, even though they lack the internal expertise required to make their outsourcing initiative successful. Organizations must ask themselves whether they have the seasoned outsourcing expertise to guide the organization through the outsourcing life cycle. Most organizational processes and procedures are based on vertical business structures that are obsolete in the new virtual outsourcing world, but they continue to view outsourcing through the eyes of individual departmental silos, each posturing to protect its own empire.

Outsourcing vendors, through dealing with numerous clients, have mastered the art of maximizing their positions with clients. They sometimes lead unsophisticated clients down a path that maximizes their own profits while creating huge barriers to exit for the client, and negatively impacting the client's business and competitive position. Using outside professionals with proven track records established through several global outsourcing initiatives is money well invested and should pay dividends throughout the outsourcing project.

External outsourcing professionals should have strong educational qualifications in business and technology, with detailed knowledge of several cross-functional disciplines, including supply management, engineering, IT, finance, quality, operations and contracts. They must have experience dealing with different cultures and have a high level of business acumen and technology knowledge in the global marketplace.

It is our hope that you view this book as advice from experienced outsourcing professionals. While much of what we have to say will not become obsolete in the near future, you should constantly check for new discoveries, innovations, changes in processes and methodologies, and any other new information to supplement materials presented here.

6. Not dedicating the best and brightest internal resources

Although experienced external outsourcing professionals can help guide organizations through the outsourcing life cycle, there is no substitute for high-performing internal candidates to form the core of the outsourcing team. These individuals understand the organization's culture, marketplace, products, processes and procedures.

Too often, organizations form their outsourcing teams using personnel at the lower range of the performance spectrum, perhaps personnel awaiting retirement or displaying problems that management has not had the courage to deal with. It is critical that candidates come from all cross-functional disciplines including finance, IT, engineering, operations, supply management, quality assurance, human resources and contracts. This cross-functional team will provide a comprehensive view of the business requirements and corresponding points of view.

Managers must be prepared to release key personnel from their day-to-day responsibilities in order to focus on the outsourcing initiative. Instead, managers are often reluctant to release high performers because they fear the impact on existing projects and that key employees will not return to their former roles. But the outsourcing initiative must take priority, even though it may very well impact existing project commitments. If the right mix of personnel is not represented in the initiative deficiencies may be uncovered after vendor selection and contract execution that will negatively impact the project.

It is critical that management recognize, compensate and articulate the organizational importance of these positions in order to attract high-performance candidates. It is equally important that these candidates believe their involvement with the outsourcing initiative will be a career enhancement and not a management wasteland assignment.

For each stage of the outsourcing life cycle, it is important to have the right team in place to oversee the effort. The composition of the outsourcing team may change over time as the organization advances through the various stages. We discuss the key ingredients for outsourcing teams at each stage in the respective chapters.

7. Rushing through the initiative

In anticipation of reaping the benefits of outsourcing, management may push the outsourcing team to rush through the organizational assessment, requirements, request for proposals (RFP), vendor selection and contract phases of the outsourcing life cycle. This is often a grievous error. Instead, organizations must follow a disciplined approach when assessing their organizational readiness for the outsourcing initiative, creating outsourcing functional requirements, developing vendor evaluation requirements, preparing a clear RFP, evaluating vendor proposals and completing contract negotiations with the best vendor.

These steps are the foundation of the outsourcing initiative. The creation, review and approval of these steps admittedly requires a huge commitment of employee resources, time and money, but rushing through them may result in conflicts in the relationship management phase, where the organization may be at the greatest risk from a financial and competitiveness perspective. In many situations we have witnessed, companies jumped into outsourcing efforts without clearly outlining critical factors such as vendor financial stability assessment, definition of service level agreements (SLAs), intellectual property rights, audit rights and dispute resolution processes.

This is just a sample of factors that must be identified and resolved in order to establish a successful outsourcing relationship, factors that we will explore in detail in subsequent chapters. During these critical outsourcing life cycle phases, the client organization is in the driver's seat and has the control to document requirements, create a detailed RFP, select vendors and propose contract terms that clearly set business requirements and expectations. Rushing through these steps can be detrimental to the initiative and, in some cases, create irrevocable damage.

8. Not appreciating cultural differences

One of the most difficult and underestimated issues facing outsourcing relationships is the impact of cultural differences between the client and vendor organizations. Client organizations scour the world for outsourcing partners, often considering vendors in India, Ireland, Israel, China, Mexico, Canada and the Philippines. Clients tend to believe that the norms, values and ethics of their vendors will be similar to their own. Once into the relationship, they realize that the vendor's views of time management, organizational structure, business approach, decision-making processes, long-term cooperation and teamwork may be very different from their own. Even if the vendor speaks English, it may be a dialect that causes key points to become distorted in the interpretation. Subtle differences in language and the context of words make for distinct semantics.

As India emerges as the global outsourcing leader, UK or US companies may not fully understand or appreciate some cultural differences. Indian companies are hesitant to tell their UK or US clients that they do not have the capabilities to execute an assignment or that they are experiencing problems during a project. The clients may not know, until the final days before a milestone, that the project is not on schedule or that there are significant cost overruns or functional deficiencies in the deliverable. This is not a function of the

Indian vendor being dishonest, but of the vendor believing it can recover in the later stages of the project and not wanting to give bad news or disappoint the client.

Many offshore outsourcing relationships get into trouble due to cultural differences where both the client and vendor organizations believe they are fulfilling their obligations, yet both sides end up being disappointed with the results and frustrated with the relationship. If these issues are not addressed and resolved in a timely manner, the relationship is destined to finger pointing, low productivity and mutual dissatisfaction. The client organization must take the time to understand the vendor's cultural milieu and educate the internal organization on these differences. This may entail developing team-building workshops with the vendor organization to help identify and bridge the cultural differences.

It is important to note that cultural differences occur even between organizations in different industries and even with organizations in the same country. Speaking to executives in Boston, Massachusetts is not exactly the same as negotiating a deal with a Texan. Moreover, cultures in IT companies differ from those in the manufacturing sector, which differ from those in the financial sector. In Chapter 5, we will discuss how to evaluate the cultural synergies between your organization and that of your vendor.

9. Minimizing what it will take to make the vendor productive

Client organizations build business processes, methodologies, tools, infrastructures, products and applications over years of an evolutionary process, but they are usually not disciplined in documenting and codifying the intellectual know-how. This knowledge is often scattered throughout all levels of the organization, from senior engineers to inventory stock personnel.

Is it realistic to believe that this know-how can readily be transferred to a vendor thousands of miles away in a different country with a different culture? Many client organizations minimize the time and effort it takes to document their know-how and to transfer it to their vendors. They set unrealistic goals for vendors in the early stages of the outsourcing relationship that create conflict and tension in the relationship before it is established.

Organizations tend to set stringent SLAs to be achieved in the early phase of the outsourcing transition. Usually, these agreements require detailed knowledge of the client's business processes and functions. Is it realistic to believe this can happen in a short time frame? Think about the impact to a company that transfers a critical business application to a vendor and then either moves or loses the internal knowledge to support the application prior to the vendor demonstrating its own knowledge of the project. This could have a devastating effect on the client's business and jeopardize the outsourcing relationship.

Client organizations must set realistic goals that allow the vendor to improve schedules, quality and costs over time, based on objective metrics mutually agreed upon by both the client and vendor organizations. Chapters 3 and 4, on strategic assessment and needs analysis, will pay particular attention to these issues.

10. Poor relationship management programs

Organizations expend resources on the outsourcing strategy, selecting vendors and negotiating contracts without realizing that this is only the ante to get into the outsourcing game. They need to understand how to manage the ongoing outsourcing relationship. The relationship management plan is the glue that holds the outsourcing relationship together. It includes descriptions of the outsourcing efforts, identification of key shareholders, schedule of activities, roles and responsibilities, budgets, performance measurements, work products, resources, required skills and knowledge, change control process, quality assurance, configuration management, communication plan and tools, equipment, facilities and security. The outsourcing relationship management plan, in effect, encapsulates the entire outsourcing relationship.

The relationship management plan should not be an afterthought following the signing of the contract, but should be developed at the first stage of the outsourcing life cycle and revised at subsequent stages. This ensures that the strategies and business structures can be molded into an objective, manageable framework that can be communicated throughout the client and vendor organizations. Chapter 8 will focus on the issues of relationship management and how to maintain and improve the quality of the outsourcing relationship as time passes and experiences with the vendor grow.

How to manage outsourcing engagements successfully

Organizations embarking on an outsourcing initiative must understand that success depends on a disciplined outsourcing life-cycle methodology requiring a commitment of skilled resources from executive management. Such a methodology will cover issues from strategy formulation, organizational assessment, planning, requirements definition, request for proposal (RFP), vendor evaluation and selection, contract formulation, negotiation to comprehensive outsourcing governance. It also depends on support from cross-functional units within the organization with a clear understanding of the organization's strategy, goals and objectives. Organizations already in an outsourcing relationship should proactively and objectively assess their relationship, identifying current and potential problems and quickly implementing corrective actions while mitigating risks.

Outsourcing is a powerful business strategy that requires a paradigm shift in the way global business is conducted. Used correctly, outsourcing can indeed deliver benefits such as cost reductions, ability to focus on core business competencies, improved quality, superior skills and capabilities, reduced time to market and competitive advantages. Organizations that make outsourcing a core competency will be well positioned for competitiveness in the global marketplace.

The next chapter outlines the outsourcing life cycle, then Chapters 3–10 explore each stage of the life cycle in detail, highlighting what to look out for, and even telling you how things might change in the future.

2 The outsourcing life cycle

There are several reasons why we discuss outsourcing using a process-driven approach. First, a process-driven approach provides you with a systemic look at the 'how-to' details of developing an outsourcing plan. Second, regardless of the nature of the outsourcing arrangement, whether it is small or large, onshore or offshore, is functional or competency-based, the steps in the process need to be followed to ensure that you are being diligent in the management of the outsourcing relationship. Third, while the components of the outsourcing process do not change over time or between projects, one thing that *should* change is the effectiveness and efficiency of the process. Through practice, experience and time an organization should increase the maturity and sophistication of how it goes through the various stages of the outsourcing life cycle. In Chapter 10 we will discuss the concept of an outsourcing management maturity model. Having a process framework provides you with a consistent view of the details of the outsourcing engagement. The framework should be used to move through outsourcing engagements and improved for better results.

The outsourcing life cycle is made up of the following stages (see Figure 2.1): (1) strategic assessment; (2) needs analysis; (3) vendor assessment; (4) negotiation and contract management; (5) project initiation and transition; (6) relationship management; (7) continuance, modification or exit strategies. Each of the stages of outsourcing has sub-components and sub-processes that need attention.

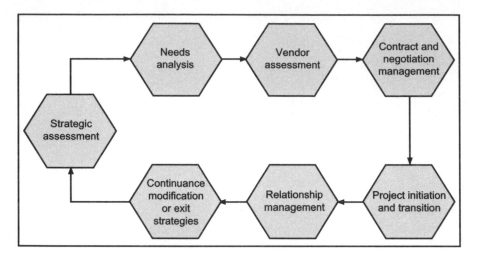

Figure 2.1 The outsourcing life cycle

Stages of outsourcing

As emphasized earlier, outsourcing must be considered as a strategic tool for the organization to employ to increase its competitiveness and performance in the marketplace. For effective outsourcing, the initiative must be evaluated in the context of the strategic posture of the organization. This strategic assessment is the focal activity in the first stage of the outsourcing process. During the strategic assessment stage, the organization makes a business case clearly identifying the intended benefits of employing outsourcing as a strategy. Doing this will require the organization to analyze its core competencies and identify areas that are suitable for outsourcing, put in place an executive team, and conduct operational, financial and risk assessments. Once a business case for outsourcing is presented and agreed upon, you are ready to get into the act of actually outsourcing.

When you have completed the strategic assessment, there might be many possible candidate areas or projects within the company that you think are ripe for outsourcing. In the next step, you must pick your battles, so to speak. This would involve prioritizing your needs and defining, at an operational level, the one or more outsourcing projects that you would like to focus on. For each such project, the next stage is to conduct a thorough needs analysis. Needs analysis is akin to a strategic assessment made at the first stage, but it is more detailed and concentrated for the specific project. Here you are looking at what the peculiarities of the given project are and how you can best articulate the requirements, evaluate the requirements by mapping them to the broader business case prepared during the strategic assessment and prepare a proposal to articulate these needs to potential vendors.

The third stage is one of soliciting, evaluating and choosing the vendor for your outsourcing needs. The vendor selection and contracting phase provides a structured framework to guide the organization through critical vendor selection and contracting activities. Choosing the right vendor is much like choosing a good partner; the chances are that if you make the right decision from the onset you will have a potentially lasting relationship, while choosing the wrong vendor could damage and thwart a well-intentioned outsourcing project.

Once a vendor is chosen, the next steps are to engage in negotiations (and renegotiations) until an agreement is reached about the details of the outsourcing work. This is followed by the composition of the outsourcing contract – the legal document that codifies the nature and scope of the business relationship. During the negotiation and contract stage the focus is on securing a legally binding deal that is documented and not just verbally arranged, and which is best for all parties involved in the outsourcing relationship.

Once all the 't's are crossed and 'i's are dotted and the business partners sign on the dotted lines, you are ready to begin the outsourcing project – the project initiation and transition phase. The stages of project initiation and transition are the most seminal stages of the outsourcing relationship – this is where 'the rubber meets the road'. This is the stage where the client organization slowly starts to relinquish control of the work to the outsourcing vendor. The initial stages of the outsourcing relationship require diligent attention to deal with emergent issues and smooth out any problems that occur. This is the stage that marks the foundation of the continued relationship; hence it is important to address problems up front rather than letting issues escalate.

After the initial stages, the outsourcing relationship should become routine enough for you to begin managing the day-to-day operations of the relationship, also called governance. The focus of this stage is to keep up to date with the outsourcing relationship. The salient activities in this stage include evaluation of the relationship, problem resolution, communications management, knowledge management and process management.

While management of the relationship is a continuous process, occasionally the client organization may face events that require it to pause and evaluate the future of the relationship. Events could be items such as new strategic alliances, changes to the vendor's business or innovations in the marketplace. An organization must evaluate its current outsourcing contract to see if its best interest lies in continuing, modifying or exiting the relationship. Choosing any one of these alternatives will call for reconnecting to the first stage of the life cycle and reconducting a strategic assessment, to repeat the life cycle.

Things to bear in mind

Before getting into each stage of the outsourcing life cycle, some critical points need to be made. First, the outsourcing process is cyclical and it is important to follow through on each stage in the prescribed manner. It will be futile to omit a stage, as your organization will miss out any benefits of following a well-organized life cycle. One of the reasons why we recommend following the stages in order is that this greatly reduces difficult decision making as you move through the model. When an organization first considers using outsourcing as a strategic tool, there are an unlimited number of possibilities to analyze. Put another way, finding the right solution that works for the organization is difficult as the solution search space is seemingly vast and unlimited. However, after conducting a thorough strategic assessment of the organization and analyzing the areas that might be candidates for outsourcing, you have narrowed the solution space drastically. At the next phase, conducting a needs analysis for a project, the choices of outsourcing are further narrowed. Similarly, after conducting vendor assessments you are left with an even narrower search space, and ultimately you choose the right set of vendors for your task. Skipping through the stages is not a wise move, nor is doing them simultaneously; each stage contributes to the next stage, building synergy into the life cycle.

Second, each stage of the outsourcing process, except for the last one on choosing to continue, modify or exit the relationship, must be conducted independent of the stage that follows it. Why is this important? Simply because it is not beneficial to conduct a stage with a preconceived answer on what you will do at a future stage. Put another way, you do not just want to go through the process if you already know the answer, or worse, tweak the process to arrive at a preconceived answer. For instance, when conducting the needs analysis, you should not be restricted by a particular vendor's offering (this will be part of the later vendor-assessment stage). You must formulate the needs for the outsourcing project, independent of any vendor, and then use the needs to choose the vendor. It is futile to engage in a process whereby you define your needs to meet the offerings of a vendor. Only in the last stage of the outsourcing life cycle, when making a decision on continuing, modifying or discontinuing the relationship, do you need to look at both the prior stage (relationship management) and the future stage (strategic assessment) to make an effective decision.

Finally, mastering the outsourcing life cycle is both a science and an art. The science part comes from well-defined principles that need to be followed for success in outsourcing. These include not rushing through the process, knowing where you are before engaging in negotiating, paying attention to communication and problem resolution during the project initiation phase, managing knowledge to improve the process, and many other details, which we will make clear in subsequent pages. Given these general principles, management is often an art. What works in one situation may not work in another. The job of the manager is to visualize and extrapolate patterns in diverse situations and work out how best to tailor existing principles to meet the new context. Hence, as with any art, only practice will make one perfect. Outsourcing is not a spectator sport and in order to learn and become a master, you must, in addition to reading this book, get your hands dirty and work through the details, over and over again.

3 Strategic assessment

This chapter examines whether outsourcing is a strategy your organization should pursue. Too often, managers and executives get excited about buzzwords – total quality management, business process reengineering, executive support systems, knowledge management and e-commerce, to name a few. Each of these terms has spun off entire management consulting practices and consulting organizations. Consultants are the first to push buzzwords! These buzzwords become a fancy and lead to the feeling, 'If X thinks it good and is spending billions on it, why aren't we?' or 'We need to embrace the idea because our competitor has'. Making decisions to pursue strategies just because someone else has done so is to relegate management thinking to the way adolescents compare possessions – 'If Jack has it, so must I'.

Every organization is unique in its value proposition, asset composition, processes, people and products. Hence, each organization needs to evaluate any new strategy seriously, in its own context, before investing in it. Consider what happened with the internet or e-commerce hype. The internet hype, also called the dot.com craze, crashed in early 2000. Most organizations and venture capitalists saw their fortunes disappear. The market adjusted its valuations of companies to reflect basic economic principles and this led to a sharp fall in stock prices.

While most companies witnessed the negativities associated with the dot.com craze, there were some organizations that took advantage of the situation. Consider the case of Amazon.com or Google.com. Both these organizations have become dominant players in their industry. Why? They had a strong business model and an uncompromising strategic focus. Similarly, the critical determinant of Dell Computers' success was its ability to build a well-oiled supply chain management system by exploiting the internet's potential for information sharing and task coordination. Other success stories of traditional brick companies that were able to revolutionize their product offerings and sales channels by exploiting the internet include Barnes & Noble and Wal-Mart. These organizations had in place the necessary back-end infrastructure services needed to complement their activities on the internet. They were hence well positioned to exploit the new functionality of the internet and use it in sync with their complementary assets and infrastructures. In comparison to these select few success stories, there were thousands of dot.com failures, or 'dot.bombs'. One reason why many dot.coms failed is quite simple – jumping on the bandwagon without appropriate strategic assessment. Organizations utilized their resources to develop sophisticated websites meant to promote online sales, but they did not have the necessary back-end infrastructure to handle the orders coming in, nor adequate security measures to prevent fraudulent transactions. In the same vein, venture capitalists pumped money into technology solutions without thinking about the business value of such investments.

More recently, the concept of outsourcing has been bantered around executive circles, popular press and news media. There are horror stories from executives who did not undertake outsourcing endeavors with due diligence. Consider the case of the US Federal Bureau of Investigation (FBI) and their attempts to develop a case management system, Virtual Case File, to track criminals and terrorists. The FBI scrapped their project in February 2004, after spending US $170 million. The FBI had outsourced the development of the system to Science Applications International Corporation (SAIC). According to the FBI, SAIC failed to deliver an acceptable system based on initial requirements and budget. While there are many reasons for this failure, one of the predominant reasons is lack of effective management oversight over the project and the external contractor. Currently, the FBI is exploring the prospects of purchasing commercially available off-the-shelf software to meet its requirements. For the FBI, having a case management system represented a core need; they needed the technology to conduct their primary job. One would expect that outsourcing efforts that involve core competencies would be the best managed. Just imagine what happens to outsourcing projects that involve auxiliary needs!

While the FBI failures are magnificent and public, there are also many failures that have been less public, but nonetheless serious. A major technology organization that one of us consulted for spent over US $5 million on a system maintenance project, only to bring the work back in-house after nine months of failed effort. To add to the financial losses, the organization had to also deal with a knowledge loss issue here, since, during the initial periods of the outsourcing project, it downsized its IT department and several senior managers quit their posts. As a result, when the work had to be brought back in-house, the experienced staff was lacking. The organization was forced to re-hire some members of its original workforce as consultants, thus paying them an added premium for their knowledge – all in all, an outsourcing catastrophe.

Horror stories like these need not be the norm. Outsourcing efforts can be fruitful and beneficial, if they are properly planned from the onset, with conducting a strategic assessment of the organization being the first, seminal step. The focus of this chapter will be on helping you make a strategic assessment about whether outsourcing is a suitable strategy for your organization to pursue. Not all areas of a business are candidates for outsourcing, nor are all areas in an immediate hurry to be outsourced. If it emerges that outsourcing is a strategy for you to consider, we will highlight mechanisms by which you can decide what processes or projects are candidates for outsourcing. It is important for any organization to take the time to consider outsourcing through a strategic lens instead of diving in blindly and having deep regrets later on. The goals of conducting a strategic assessment are as follows:

1. To develop a clear vision of outsourcing, setting tangible goals and objectives.
2. To determine how outsourcing fits into the overall business strategy.
3. To select and engage executive sponsors for the outsourcing endeavor.
4. To identify the key functions and processes suitable for outsourcing.
5. To determine whether the engagement should be onshore, near-shore or offshore.

While conducting a strategic assessment, the organization also needs to carry out the following:

1. Determine its organizational challenges.
2. Develop a mission and vision to make outsourcing work.
3. Identify risks and mitigations.
4. Identify strategies and tactics to maximize outsourcing value.
5. Communicate the results of the strategic assessment phase to key stakeholders.

The majority of outsourcing failures can be traced back to organizations that short-change or eliminate this critical strategic assessment, thereby failing to lay a solid foundation to make objective, data-driven outsourcing decisions.

Four elements of strategic assessment

The goal of the strategic assessment is to examine the current and analyze the future strategic position of the organization to understand where outsourcing as a strategy fits in. It is during this stage that the organization needs to understand both the pros and cons of using outsourcing as a strategy. An analysis of the pros and cons, and the fit – does outsourcing as a strategy fit the business needs? – will form the foundation of the outsourcing plan. Failure to lay this solid foundation in place will result in questionable outcomes in the future stages of the outsourcing life cycle. As a simple example, consider what would happen if you incorrectly analyze a particular function of your organization as being a candidate for outsourcing. Using this incorrect information, you move through the needs analysis, vendor selection, negotiating and contracting phases and then eventually turn this misinformation over to the vendor. You have just wasted enormous effort owing to an incorrect up-front assessment for which you will have to pay heavily. Eventually, you will have to bring this work back in-house and pay substantial costs for the error.

The four major elements of the strategic assessment phase include: business-value assessment, operational assessment, financial assessment and risk assessment (see Figure 3.1). The outcome of these four assessments is the outsourcing business case and recommendation. We will now walk through each of the major elements.

Figure 3.1 Four elements of strategic assessment

Business-value assessment

The business-value assessment involves three stages: analysis of the organization's core competencies, setting up an executive sponsor team to oversee the outsourcing project, ensuring that the outsourcing plan is aligned with the current and future overall business strategy (see Figure 3.2).

Core competencies

During the business-value assessment, organizations must examine their business to decide what their core competencies are. Many organizations struggle to determine this true focus of their business capability objectively. Core competencies are the combinations of special skills, proprietary technologies, knowledge, information and unique operating processes and procedures that are integrated into the organization's products and services and are unique differentiators for the organization's customers.

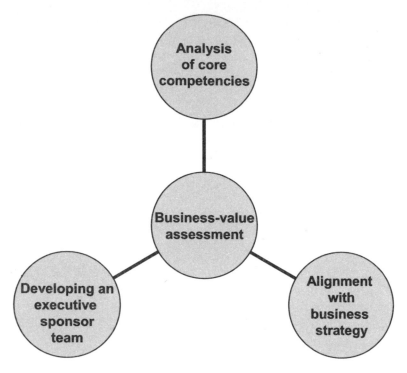

Figure 3.2 Elements of business-value assessment

Consider the case of Dell Computers. What is its core competency? Supply chain management. Dell does not physically manufacture computers; instead, it acts as an integrator and manager of the computer manufacturing process. Dell has a network of suppliers who work on various components of the computer and through the use of information technologies it is able to coordinate actions between manufacturers so as to deliver computers to its customers. What would happen if Dell loses its supply chain management competency? The company would lose many of its customers, since it would no longer be able to provide them the edge they look for, and its competitors would start taking pieces of its market share. If you could not customize your computer, have it delivered for a price less than what you find at retail, and in a reasonable time frame, then why shop with Dell? You might as well buy from your local computer retail outlet. A core competency is hence crucial in preserving the longevity and performance of any organization.

Table 3.1 Competencies

Core competencies	Non-core competencies
Are integrated into the organization's products and services	Are required for the daily operations of the business
Differentiate the organization from its competitors	Indirectly impact the products and services of the organization

In comparison to the core competencies, every organization has in place non-core competencies, also called auxiliary, peripheral, support or operational capabilities. These capabilities help keep the business afloat by aiding the completion of daily operations. For example, most organizations have competencies in the areas of accounting or financial management. Without these, the organization would not be able to conduct its daily operations. Non-core competencies differ from core competencies in two important respects. First, they do not help differentiate the organization from the others in the marketplace. Second, they do not directly impact the organization's products and services. The financial management competency of an organization will directly impact how an organization spends its cash reserves and handles its other financial assets, which may, in turn, affect the future of the organization, and through this the products and service offerings. In comparison, a supply chain management competency, if it is a core competency as with Dell Computers, will directly affect the delivery of products and services.

Once an organization has mapped out its competencies and categorized them as core and non-core, it is ready to think about which ones are candidates for outsourcing. We will discuss the details of choosing outsourcing candidate projects in the next chapter and also in the operational assessment section of this chapter. An organization must be mindful about the type of competency it plans to outsource – core or non-core. In our experience, it is best to start with outsourcing non-core processes and improve the maturity of the outsourcing practice in the organization, before crossing the chasm to outsourcing core competencies. Compared to the outsourcing of core competencies, outsourcing non-core competencies, while a serious challenge, has lower risks and consequences in terms of negativities that might materialize if the project goes sour.

Contributions of the executive sponsor team

To add credibility to the outsourcing initiative

To provide knowledge and foresight about the strategic issues facing the organization

To act as integrators to get required personnel involved in the initiative

---

Executive sponsor team

A core component of conducting a business-value assessment is to have the right team in place to conduct the assessment – the executive sponsor team. It is vital that organizations have a dedicated *executive-level* team that sponsors the outsourcing program. Executive-level teams can make several critical contributions to the strategic assessment process. First, they will add credibility to the outsourcing initiative. Most of an organization's staff looks to their executives' words and actions for guidance on what is important and what is not. Hence, without active involvement from key executives, the outsourcing program will lack enough credibility to get anywhere. An executive-level team can act as the sponsor by rallying support for the initiative.

Second, an executive-level team will have the knowledge and vision of the strategic issues facing an organization. Hence, they will be able to examine outsourcing through the lens of their perspective and vision of the future of the organization, while also filtering each topic at a high level. This is exactly what is needed to conduct the strategic assessment, especially when conducting the business-value assessment. Core competencies of an organization today may not be core competencies tomorrow, nor will they definitely fit into an organization's future strategic plans. Foresight about where the company is headed is found in the minds of the senior executives; seldom is this captured by members several levels down from the executive branch. It is therefore important to get these people involved, so that you craft out an outsourcing strategy that is feasible both in the present and the future.

Third, executives have an integration capability that is also critical. Senior-level executives dictate the schedules and tasks of their key personnel. One of the benefits of having such control is the fact that members of their teams can be relieved of their current assignments to work with other employees on the outsourcing business-value assessment, or other types of assessment, if needed. Without executive-level sponsors for an initiative, moving employees between tasks will result in disagreements between project managers.

During the strategic assessment, the outsourcing team is formed including executive sponsorship, an outsourcing team leader and representatives of all groups impacted by the proposed outsourcing initiative. Although this can vary from project to project, typical representation includes: executive sponsor, outsourcing team leader, project management, contracts/legal, finance, information systems, procurement, human resources, engineering, operations, quality and customer service and representatives from the end-user community. The goal is to get a wide perspective from multiple disciplines and identify critical success factors and problem areas that will be the foundations for compiling a comprehensive business case for outsourcing.

The outsourcing team will be responsible for the following areas:

1. Defining and documenting key business objectives and outcomes.
2. Identifying the products and services that are candidates for outsourcing.
3. Developing an understanding of the external marketplace, including the vendor's capabilities and how that can be used to help meet the organization's business objectives.
4. Clarifying roles and responsibilities.
5. Leading and managing change.
6. Defining the organizational design and culture that will be required to achieve its outsourcing objectives successfully.

This comprehensive accountability means, in effect, that the outsourcing team is responsible for creating the outsourcing business case. We will discuss the business case towards the end of this chapter. Should the organization choose to follow through on outsourcing – ie it has conducted the strategic assessment and is ready to begin the outsourcing life cycle – the outsourcing team is responsible for the initial management of the outsourcing process by determining how the organization will manage the overall outsourcing relationship. This entails managing the overall outsourcing project plan, developing realistic and objective schedules and milestones, evaluating and approving the vendor's proposed plans and suggesting changes to minimize risks. The team also needs to consider how to integrate the vendor's plans into internal functions such as IT, engineering, quality, finance, procurement, project management, customer service, operations and contracts, as well as to track and monitor the overall outsourcing business plan.

Alignment with the business strategy

The last component of the business-value assessment is to examine the organization's business strategy. This includes outlining its current business strategy and how this strategy may change in the future. Seldom do organization strategies remain static or permanent. Innovations in the marketplace, new customer needs, new competitors, new regulations, etc all have a dynamic impact on organization strategies. When considering whether to outsource or not, it is important for the organization to outline its strategies, both current and future. Not doing so will lead to an outsourcing effort that may negatively impact the organization's overall growth strategy or can lock an organization into a path for a long time, thus limiting its range of strategic direction. Consider a simple example. If the overall strategy of a technology organization is to move from selling software on CD ROMs to a digital model where customers can download the software directly from the internet for a lower cost, structuring an outsourcing contract for CD ROM production will be in conflict with the overall strategy. Backing out of a signed contract is never a pleasant deal as there are always early-termination clauses that are detrimental to the client organization.

Organizations need to ask several questions to ensure alignment between outsourcing and the business strategy. First they must ask:

How will outsourcing fit into our overall business strategy?
Is outsourcing going to help us improve our core competencies?
Is outsourcing going to help us source out auxiliary tasks so that we can focus more attention on core competencies?

If outsourcing is going to be used to complement the organization's core competencies by gaining access to knowledge and expertise residing in an external organization, it must make sure that it is collaborating or sourcing to recognized industry leaders and those that constantly innovate and come up with new practices. However, if outsourcing is going to be used to take over auxiliary services that do not have a direct impact on the organization's business strategy, it may be less inclined to pay a high premium for cutting-edge knowledge and expertise. The organization's interest here is to find an external vendor who will be able to meet its needs with minimal disruptions and overheads to its business.

Second, organizations must ask:

Is outsourcing going to be used in a short-term or long-term project?

If the organization can visualize a clearly charted road into the future, then it may be beneficial to plan a long-term outsourcing engagement. As long as the organization is sure about long-term plans, a long-term engagement will help it secure discounts and negotiate a better deal. Put another way, a long-term outsourcing contract is ideal if the organization expects to be doing the same thing in the future. However, if it is dynamic, and constantly evolving, like most high-tech companies, the chances are that it does not know what the future holds. Executives may make intelligent guesses about the future and may have plans, but those will change depending on dynamic market factors, among others. In this case, getting into a long-term deal may actually cripple the organization by making it inflexible, unable to respond to change or realign its business focus. It may even cost the organization its future, if it is truly handicapped and cannot innovate or change existing relationships to meet new business realities. Moreover, since alignment today need not be alignment tomorrow, changes to the current outsourcing relationship are going to be necessary. A short-term outsourcing project is beneficial in this scenario, as it involves a dynamic strategy, where alignment must happen in real-time.

Third, organizations must ask:

What is the underlying business argument for considering outsourcing?

To answer this question, one must be able to state clearly the internal and external factors facing the business and their impact. Why does outsourcing make business sense? We recommend that the answer to this question be prepared as though the organization were approaching the bank for a major loan or asking its shareholders their opinions on issuance of new shares. The answer must be concrete, clearly defensible, based on objective information, and should stand up to external scrutiny, for example from shareholders, creditors, etc. The answer to the question of whether outsourcing makes business sense will be written up in the outsourcing business case, which we will discuss towards the end of this chapter.

Internal factors that can lead an organization to consider outsourcing include:

- obsolescence of certain areas or stagnation in growth: an area that was once growing, even booming, and contributing to the overall business strategy, has receded to become more auxiliary, diverting focus from other growing areas;
- maturity of certain areas: areas where things are always in a state of flux during the initial stages, but over time, processes get systematized and become routine and can be conducted in an automated fashion with minimal effort;
- efforts to centralize a given function: an organization is attempting to centralize a function that is currently disparately spread out through the organization as seen in the emergence of centralized purchasing departments;
- change in business strategies: perhaps the company wants to phase out a given line of products and services and hence wants to begin outsourcing its management to a third party;
- higher cost savings and improved performance: more efficient and effective outcomes are likely when third parties can do the job better than an organization is currently doing it, and do it more economically.

External factors that might lead an organization to consider outsourcing include:

- emergence of new businesses: before the rise of companies that did payroll processing many companies handled this task internally; today external businesses exist that are superior at executing the task;
- rise of qualified talent pool in foreign locations: outsourcing of manufacturing may have led the way in utilization of foreign labor, but today outsourcing of knowledge work is also fostered by a rich and ever-expanding global talent pool of knowledge workers;

- innovations in the marketplace: innovations are normally disruptive and can call for changes in a company's mode of operations – examples include the rise of the internet and the associated sophistication of collaborative functionalities that have opened up new avenues for global collaboration and distributed work.

In order to come up with the right business case, and also to align the outsourcing initiative to the organization's current and future position properly, it is important to get the senior executives of the companies involved; which explains the earlier point of creating an executive sponsor team. The executives need to think about where the organization will be headed five or ten years from today. Doing so will draw attention to areas that are most likely to undergo changes in the future and need to be flexible. Long-term outsourcing contracts will not be ideal for these areas. Likewise, the organization may be able to identify areas that are getting stagnant or where the growth rate has declined. Maybe the organization is under pressure to lower costs in these areas, in order to be the lowest priced provider in a saturated marketplace. Here, the organization may be interested in structuring a long-term contract to take advantage of the outsourcing vendor's economies of scale.

All in all, the business-value assessment must look to providing guidance on how outsourcing would meet the organization's strategic directions, in terms of both its competencies and its strategies. To do this successfully will require participation and support from executive sponsors, a point we need to emphasize time and again.

Operational assessment

In the operational assessment of your organization, you must determine its operational baseline, including its process capabilities. You will need to know whether your organization has mature process capabilities to support the proposed outsourcing initiatives. Similarly, you will need to know whether there are established methodologies to measure performance of the proposed outsourcing initiative and benchmarking data in place to assess the maturity of the organization as well as the competitiveness of the vendor's proposal. It is during this phase that the organization must be able to answer the questions

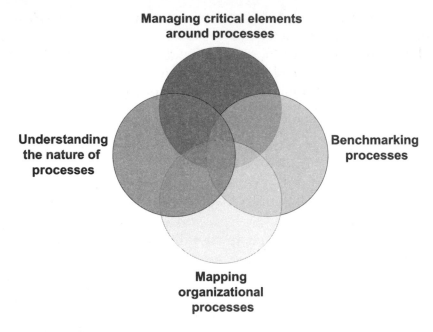

**Managing critical elements
around processes**

**Understanding
the nature of
processes**

**Benchmarking
processes**

**Mapping
organizational
processes**

Figure 3.3 Elements of operational assessment

regarding the supportability of its operations, including: Does the organization understand all the related internal and external dependencies across its entire business enterprise, as well as the internal and external impact associated with the proposed outsourcing initiative? Outsourcing normally involves moving one or more processes to an external vendor. It is hence important to know the nature of the processes before they are outsourced. This is the focus of the operational assessment. The operational assessment involves (1) mapping organizational processes; (2) understanding the nature of processes; (3) benchmarking processes and (4) managing critical elements around processes (see Figure 3.3). In this chapter, we will only cover the operational assessment at a high level; the next chapter will dig deeper into its intricacies.

Mapping organizational processes

The first component of such an assessment is to have a map of the current organizational processes. A process is a smaller unit of analysis compared to a competency – ie a competency can be made up of one or more processes. In order to create a map of organizational processes, executives must have a list of all processes and their definitions. It is important to be holistic and take a comprehensive view of organizational processes when creating the list. Leaving one or more processes out, especially in the domains where outsourcing is being considered will be costly, as it will result in an incomplete plan.

Next, you must be able to map the interconnections between the processes in terms of dependency. For instance, in examining a supply chain system you know that shipping the product (a process) can only come after the product is ready to be shipped – a temporal dependency. There may also be spatial dependencies where two processes must work in conjunction with one another to produce an output. The two processes are linked with one another in a concurrent manner here, as they must both work in an integrated fashion. An example of such a process would be where you need to make a proposal for a consulting project. This task would require individuals from marketing, new product development, legal and finance, to work together to create the proposal. Finally, you can have evolutionary dependencies, where smaller processes are combined or evolve to create bigger processes. For example, writing each chapter of this book is a process, which gets evolved into the process of writing the entire book.

It is important to understand the issues involved in outsourcing each type of process and pay attention to the peculiarities of each type of dependency (a point we will examine in greater depth in Chapter 4 on needs analysis). It is important to visualize the interrelation between processes, as this will give an indication of which processes are bundled and whether the bundle is a core or non-core competency. Bundles of processes are common in any discipline and unless executives visualize the bundle, they may naively decide to outsource one component – a single process in the bundle – without accounting for its effect on the other processes that must depend on it.

Nature of processes

The second component of the operational assessment is to identify the maturity of processes. Here the basic question is: How structured is a given process? A structured process, just like a structured problem, is easier to tackle than an ill-structured process and, like any problem, any process can get structured with time and experience. For instance, the first time we go to make a consulting bid on a project we have to tackle a rather ill-structured problem. However, over time and through experiences with multiple consulting assignments, the once ill-structured problem will become structured and we will be able to parse through the various stages in an automated format. It is important to identify the maturity of each process for the simple reason of knowing where the organization currently stands. It will be a difficult and futile proposition to try outsourcing a process that we do not know how to define, nor have an idea of how it is linked to the other processes and, even worse, how to articulate in a structured manner as it is an immature process.

To get a better grasp of the different types of process you may have in the organization, we suggest segmenting them. An organization must be able to segment its processes into a number of dimensions. Figure 3.4 shows processes segmented into four types, based on the dimensions of process maturity and strategic value. Segmenting processes in this manner allows you to classify and reduce the large collection of processes into manageable chunks. Let us walk through the four types of process based on the classification scheme.

Type I processes represent the core processes of the organization's assets, but they are immature. They are of serious importance as they are the ones that differentiate the organization from its competitors in a positive way. These could be R&D processes that are being

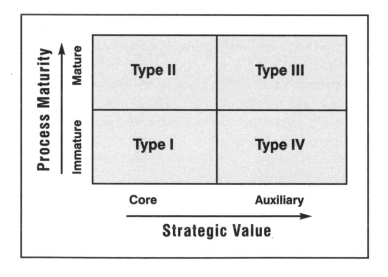

Figure 3.4 Segmenting processes

developed, new business practices being implemented, new innovations, etc. Outsourcing these processes is not a wise move in most cases, as the organization does not have enough experience in conducting them, which explains the immaturity. Moreover, as these are core processes they represent value to the organization, hence they must be protected from the external world. Consider a simple personal example. Let us say you have a new idea that you think is going to make you significantly wealthy. You have not worked out all of the details, but do have good rationale to invest in this idea. What are the chances you will share this with an outsider? Low, because you do not know whether the outsider will take advantage of this idea and commercialize it faster than you can.

Type II processes are mature processes that represent the core competencies of the organization. Outsourcing them will be an easier sell than with Type I processes, as you have experience in them, can easily define them, have metrics in place to manage them and have also automated them. As they are core, you must be sure about the outsourcing vendor's capabilities and your trust in their execution of the process, before you can outsource them (a point we will elaborate in Chapter 5 on vendor assessment). Since outsourcing core competencies that are mature only makes sense if the vendor is able to clearly provide superior value than exists in-house, it is important that you benchmark your organization's processes. Benchmarking processes entails identifying, understanding and adapting outstanding processes that improve organizational performance and is discussed in the following section.

Type III processes are what most of us are familiar with in terms of outsourcing. These processes are the most commonly outsourced and are characterized by processes that are mature yet auxiliary. Prime examples are payroll processing and benefits administration. Organizations have been implementing these processes since their inception – after all, we all like to get our pay slips and most of us are rational folk who will not work for free! While most organizations have been implementing these processes, they were not effective or efficient executions. This led to the creation of entire organizations that became experts in conducting these activities, such as Ceridian. Owing to simple economies of scale, having an organization that processes millions of payroll transactions will be advantageous versus one that runs only a thousand transactions.

Finally, we have Type IV processes that are auxiliary yet immature. In recent times, the outsourcing of most basic software development falls under this category. Software development processes in most organizations are immature, except in serious, global players in software development. Software projects routinely fail to deliver on their intended promises, overrun budgets and many are even abandoned before they are completed (as in the FBI example mentioned earlier). While this may be true for most organizations who are not in the software development business, there are other companies whose core processes revolve around software development, such as Infosys, TCS, Wipro, Cognizant, to name a few of the most prominent Indian software organizations. As software development is their core competency, they have matured the art of creating and deploying software. As such, many organizations are better off outsourcing their software development projects to these organizations that are better suited to execute them with consistency and maturity.

Benchmarking processes

To be successful at outsourcing processes, an organization needs to be able to evaluate its current processes. One of the reasons why you would like to outsource a process is to witness better process performance and results. You cannot do this unless you know the current performance of a process. It is essential that during the operational assessment you take the time to measure the current performance of the processes you are thinking of outsourcing, because it serves two valuable purposes.

First, it will help reveal the current performance of the process – where the organization stands today. This can be used as a baseline to measure future performances of the process. Second, measuring the process will uncover weaknesses and limitations in the current process and this will help identify expectations in terms of where you want process performance to be. Put another way, it will set the bar in terms of the level of process performance that you would like to witness after managerial interventions. This book is concerned with the managerial intervention of outsourcing. Hence, it looks at the performance levels expected from the outsourcing vendor. Obviously, it is a good thing if the vendor can achieve higher performance levels than expected; on the other hand, if the vendor is performing below your expectations or worse yet, below what the original levels of performance were, you have a problem on your hands.

Processes need to be measured by considering two types of information: objective and subjective. Objective information represents the hard facts, such as time to completion, number of errors and similar other efficiency ratios. These help evaluate the performance of a process in the context of its operations. Objective information can also be used to benchmark how your organization's process compares with other organizations'. Subjective information involves gathering perceptions about the process from the various stakeholders. These could include perceptions about the strengths and weaknesses of the process, areas for improvement, issues faced when the process is deployed, etc. Subjective information normally helps you to get deeper insights into the process. Used along with the objective information, this can help form a clear picture of where the process currently stands and what to expect in terms of improvements for the future, regardless of whether you decide to keep the process in-house or outsource it.

In the next chapter, we will talk about constructing service level agreements (SLAs). SLAs are an important ingredient when defining the outsourcing project, as they establish the agreed levels of service to which you will hold the vendor liable. One of the key areas in the operational assessment is deciding what service levels need to be in place for the products and services that are being considered for outsourcing. In developing an SLA it is important to define overall business objectives, your process methodology and the benchmarks that are used, in order to ensure that the SLA reflects a realistic picture of your current and future business requirements. It is also important to set realistic performance metrics, including targets, minimums and acceptable levels versus unacceptable performance levels. Again, you will also need to establish the organization's business requirements by defining the operating metrics indicative of business success. Organizations need to identify the metrics that have an impact on the products and services to be outsourced and the expected levels of performance that the business requires to operate upon. In addition, they need to be well defined, as well as easily monitored and managed, with the ability to measure dimensions of the product and service that include: availability, timeliness, quality, productivity and cost effectiveness.

Managing critical elements around processes

A number of critical elements make the processes of an organization go (or stop). These include the employees who execute the processes, suppliers or other business partners who provide inputs or are intermediaries in the process, regulations that govern how a process should be conducted or executed, etc. All of these elements also need to be accounted for in the operational assessment.

When a process is being selected or assessed for outsourcing, it is critical that you account for the employees who will be affected. You need to follow a similar methodology to the one described above when conducting the operational assessment for processes, with only one difference – here you are concerned with employees. You will have to create a map of the employees that make each process complete. For instance, you will need to enumerate the different functions and job positions and the interrelations and dependence among these. In addition, you will have to segment the employees. For example, if you are going to outsource the human resources function of the organization, you will have to identify the employees who may be affected – recruiters, benefits administrators, payroll administrators, etc.

Once you have identified the employees who will be affected by the outsourcing of a process, you must then identify how much of the process depends on the employee. Put another way, are the processes dependent on employee-specific interventions? If a process is fairly structured and understood, we would hope that it is not employee-specific. However, if employees have tacit knowledge and non-substitutable skills that contribute heavily to the process, then you will have a difficult time outsourcing the process, as it cannot be detached from the employee.

External partners that the organization currently has and their roles in the processes must also be accounted for. Key questions here include:

- Do you have existing contracts with business partners that will be affected should you decide to outsource a process?
- If you do, what are the costs involved in modifying existing relationships, if modification of existing contracts is an option?

These are non-trivial issues and must be assessed up front. A very profitable and sound outsourcing plan will quickly become damaging and costly if your current business partners drags you into legal battles.

Finally, you must account for governmental regulations and restrictions that affect the processes. For instance, the US government, especially the Defense Department, has very stringent rules and stipulations that dictate how its processes, if outsourced, should be carried out. Contractors for the Defense Department have to have security clearances before they will be allowed access to sensitive information. The security clearances are non-transferable from individual to individual or corporation to corporation. Hence, if a process is subject to regulations by the government in how and where it is conducted, it is very likely that outsourcing it will not be easy. It may be possible, but you must be aware of the up-front costs.

Many countries have laws against the outsourcing of work involving sensitive material such as medical and financial records of consumers. The executive sponsor team should raise these issues for discussion in the early stages of considering outsourcing. Companies can have the entire business affected if they outsource processes or competencies that are bound by legal regulations.

All told, the operational assessment deals with examining the process issues. When the operational assessment is complete, you must have a good sense of where your organization's processes stand and which ones are candidates for possible outsourcing. The operational assessment can be a daunting and time-consuming process, but is critical for organizations to assess their current state objectively and determine where they want to go in the future. The operational assessment complements the business-value assessment by digging a bit deeper into the actual processes that you may consider outsourcing. We will revisit much of the above discussion in the next chapter.

Financial assessment

Probably the most talked about reason for outsourcing is cost savings. Cost efficiency and improvement to the bottom line are important benefits of the outsourcing strategy. Much of this cost saving is realized by moving from a fixed-cost model to one of a variable cost. Consider a simple example. If an organization wanted to have an in-house shipping capability for mailing goods to its customers, it would have to

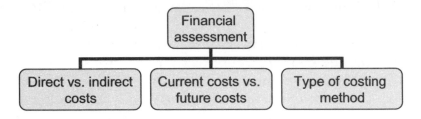

Figure 3.5 Elements of financial assessment

bear an enormous fixed cost such as a fleet of trucks, a warehouse and an information system to track shipments. These costs are fixed, because, regardless of how many products get shipped, the organization will have to pay them. Now, consider the outsourcing model, wherein the organization decides to allow DHL or FedEx to handle its logistics and shipment details. The organization's cost structure will move from one that is fixed to one that is variable. True, there is the basic yearly fee for the contract, but the rest of the expenses on the shipping and logistics will be proportionate to the number of packages shipped.

While cost effectiveness has been one of the most touted reasons for outsourcing, in our experience few companies realize the true potential of cost savings. The critical reason for this shortcoming is that organizations do not conduct financial assessment of their current processes effectively (see Figure 3.5). Hence, since they do not know how much a process costs currently, they have no solid baseline against which to compare a vendor's proposed cost. To get a true assessment for the potential of cost savings, organizations must understand their own internal costs and the different types of cost associated with outsourcing a process. The financial assessment involves direct versus indirect costs, current costs versus future costs and type of costing method (see Figure 3.5).

Direct versus indirect costs

There are two major types of cost: direct and indirect. Direct costs are usually very tangible and easy to measure, including the cost of conducting the process in terms of resource consumption (for example, how much electricity it takes to run a machine plus the cost of raw materials), employee cost (such as salaries and benefits) and general administration costs (such as administrative fees, management systems costs, capital assets costs). These costs are the ones that normally appear on any costing report or financial statement. Indirect costs are the expenses an organization has to bear but which are difficult to measure. These include items such as legal fees to develop new contracts, employee assistance and displacement fees owing to job reassignment or terminations and communications expenses. These costs are indirect, in the sense that they do not directly play a role in the process companies plan to outsource, but have an impact on the whole organization and through that impact, affect the overall cost.

In addition to direct and indirect costs, you must also be wary of the hidden costs of outsourcing. Hidden costs are less tangible in nature and in many cases difficult to measure and report. One of the major hidden costs organizations fail to appreciate is the effort involved in going through the various stages of the outsourcing life cycle. There is an enormous cost to bear in terms of staff hours, planning resources, gathering information, meetings and negotiations, etc. Other hidden costs include costs involved in conducting change management (getting support for the outsourcing effort), costs involved in managing the relationship (including the costs of resolving disputes and discrepancies, meeting with the vendors, negotiations, etc) and costs involved in contingency planning. Outsourcing efforts require an organization to devise contingency protocols to deal with negative outcomes if they materialize during an outsourcing relationship, so other hidden costs may include loss in revenue owing to disruption to the business caused by the transition, productivity loss because of low employee morale, costs associated with getting the new business partner up to speed (also called a learning curve cost), etc.

An organization *must* examine and conduct a financial assessment for each process it is considering outsourcing. Carrying out a financial assessment should include the measurement of both direct and indirect costs associated with the process. Moreover, the organization must also conduct an assessment at the macro level. By this we mean that the organization should not just isolate costs of individual processes. Financial assessments should also be made for bundles of processes, ie groups of processes that are interrelated. Looking at costs at the macro level may lead to discoveries of more indirect costs, as there will be costs involved in the integration between processes.

Current costs versus future costs

One of the activities of the financial assessment is to evaluate and estimate both the current costs of your processes and what you expect them to be in the future. Let us provide an example. Assume that your current human resource division is costing your company US$12 million per year. This cost includes the costs of all employees working in the department, the cost of the information systems required, the money spent on recruiting, payroll processing, benefits administration, etc. To gain a benefit from outsourcing, you must be able to secure a deal with a vendor that is less than your current cost of US$12 million. But how much less is enough? Is US$11.5 million enough or is US$9 million better?

The answer to this question will depend on your analysis of the indirect and hidden costs of outsourcing. You must try to secure a deal that will account for the indirect and hidden costs of outsourcing. In effect, after accounting for these costs and the current costs of the process, you can arrive at a figure that would be appropriate. Alternatively, if you are going to receive a quote from a vendor who is ready to take on the outsourcing project for a price tag of US$11 million, it may not be worth the effort, as you would probably expend US$1 million just going through the outsourcing effort.

The next point to pay attention to is the costs throughout the duration of the outsourcing process. For example, if the organization were to pay US$11 million per year for the outsourcing of the human resource function, and assuming that it enters into a five-year contract, there is a saving of around US$5 million (US$1 million per year). Cost savings over the term of the proposed outsourcing contract are good indicators of the viability of the outsourcing relationship. It is normal to have a large up-front cost for entering and creating the outsourcing relationship, but these costs should subside as the outsourcing relationship improves and matures. The important point here is that you should forecast the financial position of the outsourcing relationship over time and not take a snapshot view. And finally, you must also estimate an exit cost. Exit costs can be defined as the costs that your organization would have to bear upon the planned termination of the contract, or an unplanned termination, to move the outsourcing project back in-house or to a new vendor. These costs can be substantial and must be accounted for during the initial financial assessment. We will discuss the details of exit strategies in Chapter 6 on negotiations and contracting and Chapter 9 on continuance, modification and exit strategies.

Type of costing method

Besides understanding your organization's internal costs, you must be prepared to analyze price proposals from vendors and determine their overall competitiveness. There are two common approaches used when assessing vendors' proposals: price down and cost up. Price down compares the prices to be paid by the organization against real market prices paid by other customers who buy similar products and/or services. Cost up calculates the fair market price by simulating the vendor's costs, based on the known costs of organizations delivering similar services in-house. Price down works best when the pricing is detailed, the service or products are commodities and service providers use similar pricing models. Cost up works best for large multiservice contracts in which some products and services may have cross-subsidized others, service providers' pricing is at extremely high levels and there is insufficient competition for comparable price analysis. Your approach for conducting costing and financial assessments needs to be the same as those requested from a potential vendor, so as to enable a true comparison of figures.

To sum up, during the financial assessment organizations must prepare current cost performance that includes baseline operation costs, understand the benefits and costs associated with obtaining the desired service levels, evaluate the cost of transition and progress to an analysis of the annual cost and ROI of moving forward with the proposed outsourcing initiative.

Risk assessment

If there were no risks, there would be no need for managers. Risks and uncertainty is what management is all about. If everything were certain, and hence predictable, there would be nothing to manage. Risk is always

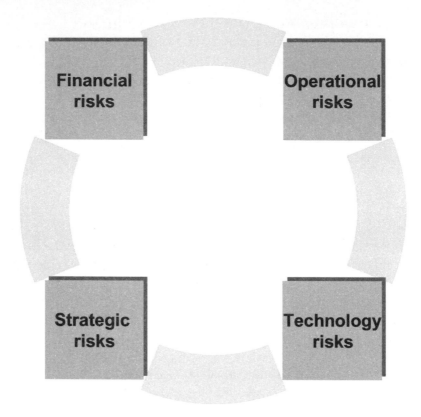

Figure 3.6 Elements of risk assessment

a factor of every project. Risk assessment takes an aggregate view of the organization and the proposed outsourcing initiative and identifies risk and associated risk mitigation strategies. When you consider that risk is associated with any project, you must segment the risk into different categories: strategic risks, operational risks, technology risks and financial risks (see Figure 3.6).

Strategic risks

Strategic risks deal with issues of interaction between the organization and the proposed vendor. Key questions include:

- Are the strategies of the two organizations compatible?
- Are the organizations' strategies in conflict and do they limit or inhibit the success of the proposed initiative?

- What is the partnering experience of both parties?
- Have they had experience and success in establishing and managing these types of relationship?
- What is the level of executive commitment? And are the executives truly supportive of the proposed initiative?
- Are they committed to providing the vision, leadership, resources and resolve to make the initiative successful?

Industry position leverage objectively assesses the relative strengths and weaknesses of both the client and vendor organizations to determine how the partnership can strengthen the competitive position of the partners. Management expertise assesses the collective management capabilities and depth of the client and vendor organizations. Seasoned outsourcing management talent is limited today and many companies struggle to attract and retain outsourcing managers. In many cases, organizations are forced to go to outside consulting firms to help them through the process. As outsourcing becomes a strategic element of an organization's overall business strategy, it will be important to build these capabilities organically in-house.

Strategic risks include intellectual property risk, which involves assessing the risk of exposing internal intellectual property to an external services provider. Companies must identify and assess their intellectual property and objectively assess the risk of exposing their property to an external service provider. Although there has been some positive movement globally in the protection of intellectual property, companies must consider the risk and recourse if their intellectual property rights are breached.

Operational risks

Operational risks address the risk of managing the internal and external operational elements of the proposed outsourcing initiatives. These risks address an array of elements such as defining the roles and responsibilities of the management and operation staff, and determining process, procedure, methodology and mismatch between the buyer and service provider organizations.

Other operational risks include staff transition, retention and attrition rates. In India today, staff attrition has increased well over 20 per cent recently in many of the IT services, a rate unheard of a few years ago. Training is a concern and plans need to be put in place to address product, process and technology training requirements. In many cases, cultural issues can be a major obstacle in the success of outsourcing initiatives. It is never easy to integrate different cultures with different norms and values. Both the buyer and service provider must address the potential cross-cultural issues and plan on conducting team building and cross-cultural training.

Technology risks

The technology risk assessment identifies the organization's technology support attributes. This assessment also exposes potential risks associated with the proposed outsourcing project technology and impact on both the client and vendor organizations.

During the technology assessment, the client needs to understand the architectural approach and requirements of the proposed initiative and the impacts of these decisions through the life of the solution. Many decisions will have to be made at this time, including standardization versus customization of the proposed solution as well as regulatory compliance, security, reliability and testability of the design as human-factor considerations. It is also important to consider customer support attributes such as responsiveness, warranty, testing, upgrades, maintenance and repair, training, documentation and the overall product support methodology.

This assessment considers all the technology elements that may pose a risk, from cradle to grave. Organizations must consider security issues and determine the products and/or services for which security risk is minimal and most conducive to outsourcing. If the products and/or services to be outsourced are extremely sensitive, adequate security measures must exist to protect intellectual property and data. Also, outsourcing may not be the best option if there is a huge cost associated with bringing the product and/or service back in-house if outsourcing does not work. Alternative options should be explored, such as keeping the work in-house.

Financial risks

The financial risk assessment defines and baselines all internal costs and financial system maturity levels. It also identifies all financial risks associated with moving forward with the proposed outsourcing initiative. This can include the financial stability of both the client and potential vendor. The costs of moving forward with the proposed outsourcing initiative must be considered, including internal versus external cost analyses for cost elements such as human resources costs, development costs, production costs, training costs, travel costs, transition costs, communications and management costs. Also, the organization will need to assess its internal financial systems and processes to determine their maturity levels and put together analyses and report costs that address any system or process deficiencies.

Managing risks

The goal of risk assessment is to make executives aware that outsourcing is a risky business proposition. This is not to say that the risks cannot be managed and mitigated. However, to do this it is important that executives are first aware of the risks and their nature. Once risks are outlined, the next step involves assessing the risks. This includes assigning probabilities to each risk, indicating the likelihood of the risk materializing at all. In addition to the assignment of probabilities, executives must also assign costs that will be incurred if the risk materializes. Put another way, if the risk were to occur, how much would the organization have to shell out to manage its outcomes and get the business back to normal?

Using the list of risks, their probabilities of occurrence, and associated costs, organizations can employ various options to manage risks. First, organizations must ask themselves how much risk they are willing to bear. Answering this question will give a sense of what risks they are even considering managing and what risks they do not want to undertake. For risks that organizations do not want to undertake or manage, they may have to find sources of insurance or hedge these risks or abandon outsourcing as a strategy. To take the example of a software project, if an organization does not want to undertake risks in terms of technology disruptions, it could choose to run two versions of an information system for a given period, one that is its existing system and one that is created by the vendor. It can continue this until it is satisfied with the quality of the new system and ready to rely on it solely. Second, to manage risks organizations must identify risk mitigation strategies. These strategies or interventions need to be stated clearly in the outsourcing contract when entering into the agreement. For instance, if loss of data is viewed as a high probability event and one that is costly, the organization should ensure that its vendor has appropriate disaster recovery and backup procedures in place to counter this risk. Finally, a contingency plan or backup solution must be developed. For severe risk, ie risks that have a high probability of occurring and are costly if they occur, contingency plans must be in place. These plans should help organizations decide what actions need to be executed should these risks materialize.

Integrating the four risk elements – the business case

After the organization has completed a thorough internal assessment of the risks associated with a successful outsourcing program, the outsourcing team must finalize and submit the outsourcing business case. As discussed earlier, the outsourcing business case is a detailed plan that documents the proposed outsourcing initiative from both a strategic and operational perspective. It gives executive management and key stakeholders an objective assessment in order to determine the feasibility of moving forward with the proposed outsourcing initiative. A business case normally includes the following components:

- Executive summary: contains the high-level view of the outsourcing strategy. In particular, it summarizes each of the individual components of the business case.
- Case for outsourcing: outlines the rationale. In particular, it explores the business-value elements of outsourcing efforts.
- Executive sponsorship: highlights key personnel who endorse and sponsor the effort and their roles and responsibilities in terms of making the effort successful.
- Objectives, purpose and scope: covers the operational assessment, specifically highlighting the areas in which outsourcing would be an appropriate strategy to pursue and for what reason.
- Planned outcomes and benefits, cost and benefit analysis: explores details of the financial and risk assessments by highlighting the expected contributions of outsourcing to the firm.
- Risk, mitigation and assumptions: outlines the findings of the risk assessment analysis.

- Operational details: contains details such as the project plan, resource management issues, costs and schedules, communications plans and roles and responsibilities. These will be fleshed out upon completion of a thorough needs analysis, which we will discuss in the next chapter.

Each part of the outsourcing business case must be clearly articulated and comprehensive. If you cannot clearly state the issues, the chances are that you will not be able to manage them clearly. This document should be the starting point for the rest of the outsourcing life-cycle process. We will explore how to define the needs of the outsourcing project in the next chapter.

Conclusion and checklist

The goal of this chapter was to help you conduct a strategic assessment of where your organization stands prior to committing to outsourcing. The old adage, 'A stitch in time saves nine' holds true here. As the first step, the strategic assessment is the foundation for organizations to determine their overall readiness to embark on an outsourcing initiative. A detailed analysis of an organization's strategic, operational, financial and risk elements provides a true assessment of its current baseline as well as its future objectives so that it can begin its outsourcing project. Organizations that invest and follow this disciplined assessment process will exponentially increase their likelihood of a successful outsourcing engagement.

The focus of strategic assessments should be on minimizing common errors: business objectives not clearly defined, outsourcing objectives misaligned with business strategies, poor documentation of operational processes and their intricacies, the inability to provide full and complete internal costing, poor construction of cost benchmarks and inadequate risks assessment. The following key questions provide a checklist to ensure that you have conducted an adequate strategic assessment:

- What is your current business strategy and future business strategy?
- What are the areas of core competencies of your business? How might these evolve in future?

- Is there an adequate executive sponsor team to lead the outsourcing initiative?
- What are the internal and external factors that are driving the need for outsourcing?
- How does outsourcing contribute to your business strategy?
- Do you have an adequate understanding of your processes, the manner in which the processes are mapped, and have you benchmarked them?
- What are the financial assessments in terms of direct and indirect and current and future costs and revenues of engaging (or not engaging) in the outsourcing effort?
- Do you understand and appreciate the risk element of outsourcing and do you have strategies in place to manage risks?
- Is there a documented and acceptable business case for outsourcing?

4 Defining your needs

After completing the strategic assessment, you will have identified areas of your organization that are suitable for outsourcing. The challenge now is to pick one or more of these areas and define the needs of the project. Strategic assessments are business cases for the entire organization in terms of which areas are suitable for outsourcing and which are not. This chapter focuses on needs analysis in order to build business cases that are specific for one or more outsourcing projects. Going through details of the operational-assessment process will be a major undertaking in defining needs.

Defining the needs of an outsourcing project represents a seminal step in the outsourcing life cycle, as it is the statement of needs that gets transferred to the vendor, decides the outcomes of the efforts and sets the stage for evaluation of the outsourcing project. Without appropriate care in defining the needs of the effort, only one outcome is assured – a disaster. A disaster can occur due to expectation failures, such as expectation failures between the client and vendor due to lack of common understanding of needs, expectation failures between the product or service delivered and what was originally conceptualized and expectation failures between the stakeholders' expectations of the effort and what was delivered. For example, if the outsourcing project costs the organization more than it was costing when done in-house, there is a problem. Another possible scenario is when the client expected to get X and received Y. The burden is on the client to state clearly the needs of the outsourcing project, as without this articulation confusion and ambiguity will plague the outsourcing relationship.

To be effective, needs definition must be conducted without undue influence from vendors. As client, *you* must be in-charge of defining your own needs and getting them right! Do not allow your vendors to define your needs for you – this will be dangerous and costly! Our recommendation is that you do not even talk to vendors before clearly articulating your needs and agreeing on them. We begin this chapter by discussing how to go about choosing the process we would like to outsource. Next, we discuss the concepts of total outsourcing and multi-sourcing. Each of these concepts has bearings on the type of outsourcing project we would like to engage in. Following this, we discuss the two main deliverables from the process: the request for proposals (RFP) and the statements of work (SOWs). We conclude the chapter by looking at common errors made by organizations during the needs definition process.

An in-depth look at operational assessment

The previous chapter discussed some of the high-level details of conducting an operational assessment; in this chapter we will dig a bit deeper into the process. While your organization must conduct an operational assessment as part of the overall strategic assessment, it must also conduct operational assessments in a detailed manner on each process that you plan to outsource.

Critical questions of needs analysis

To outsource or not?
What to outsource?
Does it make business sense to outsource the process?
Can you outsource the process?
Can you measure the process?

To outsource or not?

A few years ago, many would have advocated that it is best only to outsource non-core competencies. This advice was given regardless of whether one was involved with onshore, near-shore or offshore outsourcing efforts. The reasoning behind this is quite simple – you do not want anyone else doing something as valuable to your business as core competencies, and, if problems occurred, potentially your business could be closed down. Many organizations started by outsourcing practices such as human resource management, in particular remuneration and employee benefits administration. Outsourcing of this practice was considered non-core and one that could be outsourced with minimal disruption to the organization's customers.

Today, as a testament to the maturity of outsourcing practices, even core functions are being outsourced. Practices such as product engineering, R&D and customer service management, once considered the core competencies of many organizations, are being outsourced. Outsourcing core competencies is obviously a more challenging task than outsourcing non-core competencies. Outsourcing of core competencies requires greater trust in the outsourcing vendor, greater oversight in terms of coordination and control of the outsourced project and extensive reliance on the vendor's ability to innovate and be a leader in its market space.

Some of the large pharmaceutical companies have outsourced portions of their R&D to start-up biotechnology firms, university research centers and other organizations. Why? At first glance, one might think this is a risky and unintelligent proposition. After all, pharmaceutical companies have to invest billions in R&D for discovery of new drugs to cure ailments and it is through these discoveries and their successful commercialization that they are able to stay in business.

Actually, outsourcing packets of their competency provides the pharmaceutical companies with several advantages. First, it helps them access knowledge that is not available inside the firm by getting access to researchers who are not employed on their payroll. Access to knowledge from external sources is a critical reason to forge an outsourcing relationship. Second, it lowers their risk exposure. If the organization has a contract with another independent firm to conduct work on a particular drug-discovery project, should things go wrong with the drug discovery, especially during the initial stages of testing and re-testing, the pharmaceutical company can insulate itself from the bad news and limit its losses to the value of the contract. On the other hand, if the bad news emerged from one of the company's own laboratories, this news could have a lasting and long-term negative impact on the company's brand name.

What to outsource?

Once you decide that you would like to outsource a given set of processes, the next matter to be attended to is deciding where to focus your energies. It is here that you need to prioritize those areas identified when conducting strategic assessments to decide which of these you should focus on first. All organizations have limited resources and unlimited wants; in order to be successful at outsourcing it is very important that an organization prioritize its wants. Going through the outsourcing life cycle is a costly and time-consuming process, so it will be futile to start up multiple outsourcing projects simultaneously and have each of them compete for a small set of resources.

In order to prioritize and identify your outsourcing needs, you must revisit the list of processes you created and the map of process interdependencies. The map will tell you which processes can be outsourced in isolation, and which need to be outsourced as a bundle, ie a collection of multiple processes. For example, if you are planning to outsource the benefits administration function of the human resources department, how tightly coupled is this with the payroll functions? Being aware of these interdependencies up front will help you decide how best to go about outsourcing.

When managing process interdependencies, you can take one of two approaches: the top-down or bottom-up approach. Under the top-down approach you decide to outsource a process and in doing so agree to outsource the sub-components or sub-processes. For example, in the case of the human resource project, you could decide that you would like to outsource the entire human resource function and hence automatically need to outsource the sub-functions of benefits and payroll administration. The bottom-up approach calls for you to focus attention on sub-processes and then move upward to complete outsourcing of the major process.

The critical issue to ensure here is the separability of operations. Can you separate one process from the rest in order to work on it without disruption to the overall system? If you cannot, then the process is said to be tightly coupled with the rest, which would call for the entire system to be outsourced rather than a singular function or process. If the process can be separated with minimal disruption to the overall system, then you can outsource it and keep the rest of the system intact.

Does it make business sense to outsource the process?

There are many processes that an organization may conduct that can be candidates for outsourcing to third parties, but what is the business-value argument for doing so? This is a critical question that must be answered up front, once the organization has identified processes that can be outsourced.

As guidelines, we suggest asking the following three questions:

- If you were to start your business today, would you still conduct this process internally?
- Are you so good at the execution of this process that other companies will hire you to do it for them?
- Will most of your top executives likely come from this function or have made their name or have extensive experience in this function?

If the answer to these three questions is yes, then you should not outsource the process. It obviously represents a core activity of your business that you are doing better than anyone else, hence outsourcing it will not improve the performance of the function.

In addition to these high-level questions, we recommend that you do not outsource your core functions or processes to outsiders, unless the outsiders can do them better than you can. For a product development company, outsourcing a high percentage of R&D will not be recommended as this activity can make or break the company; moreover, unless the company is getting something better than it has in-house, it risks losing its core competency or diminishing its value. Take the case of Nike, the sports apparel giant. Nike outsources the production of its shoes, jerseys and other sports goods, but not the marketing of the brand image. Similarly, if you are a management consulting company, you can outsource almost anything from human resource functions to the purchase of office supplies, but not the areas of knowledge in which you sell consulting services or the process of service delivery.

Can you outsource the process?

To recap from the previous chapter, an organization must be realistic about whether it can outsource a given process. Much of this will depend on the nature of the process, for example is it structured and well understood or is it unstructured and poorly defined? Outsourcing the former will be an easier feat to accomplish than outsourcing the latter. Moreover, as mentioned earlier, in some areas legal restrictions play a vital role in deciding what work can be outsourced and what work cannot. The outsourcing of work involving sensitive and personal information, such as medical or financial records of customers, is often restricted by law. Processes requiring access to sensitive data may be regulated and conducive to be conducted in-house rather than being outsourced. Finally, the existence of patents, copyrights or trademarks will also affect what can be outsourced and what cannot. Processes that are protected by such measures may not be candidates for outsourcing, unless the organization can guarantee that the processes will be used in strict confidence and can structure some sort of royalty-based payments for the use of the protected process.

In addition, to legal restrictions, you must ask yourself two key questions: If it were made public that you are outsourcing a given process, how would your board of directors react? How would your customers react? If you fear that your board of directors may not view the news in a positive manner, the chances are that your shareholders will have a similar reaction. The news may devalue your stock and the negative press can hurt your business. Similarly, if your customers take issue with your outsourcing a given process, it may be because they consider that to be your core competency. Put another way, the reason why they purchase your products is because they think you do the job better than your competitors. In addition, they feel that by outsourcing the process the quality of your products and services will likely suffer, and these perceptions are serious issues that need to be dealt with. One strategy is to educate your stakeholders about the nature of the outsourcing effort and convince them that outsourcing will actually benefit the customers in terms of a better product or lower prices. The other way is simple – do not outsource the process.

Can you measure your processes?

In order to evaluate the success or failure of outsourcing efforts you must have clear benchmarks and measures for how the processes are performing currently. Measuring the process performance will help you devise the appropriate service level agreements (SLAs) that you will incorporate into the statements of work (SOWs) and request for proposals (RFP). These measures will also help you choose the right vendor to meet your expectations, will make their way into the outsourcing contracts and also be used during the relationship management phase to measure the success of the relationship. As mentioned in the previous chapter, you need to gather both objective and subjective data when measuring processes and, in addition, be able to benchmark the performance of your processes against some other measures, to get a sense of how well your organization is performing in comparison to others.

There are many ways to benchmark and many entities to benchmark against. In order to benchmark, we suggest using the SWOT (strengths, weaknesses, opportunities, threats) model, in addition to comparison of objective and subjective information. For each process, first identify its strengths in relation to the object you are comparing against (see the next paragraph for comparison units). Strengths can include: superior process efficiencies and superior and differentiating process effectiveness, ease of management, low over-heads, etc. Similarly, you must outline the weaknesses of the processes, such as unstructured nature or high cost of management. Opportunities are areas where you can seek to improve the processes, and can include both those that are internal and external to the organization. For example, innovations in the marketplace that have bearings on improving the process are external sources of opportunities, while retraining employees in new methods and procedures to improve the process is an internal opportunity. Finally, you have to outline the threats. Threats include elements that your organization must guard against since they can eat away at the current strengths or increase the weaknesses of its processes. These can be viewed as critical events that have the potential to impact the conduct of the process in a negative manner. For example, if a competitor brands or secures a patent for a particular process that your organization is currently experimenting with, this could undermine your ability to leverage the process. Another example would be if key employees leave your organization. If they were responsible for the management of a given unstructured process, where much of what keeps the process in play is the knowledge possessed by these individuals, the process could be undermined.

Benchmarking can be conducted in reference to internal, competitor, industry or process information. Internal benchmarking involves comparing the performance of the process to similar processes found within the same organization. This is a common practice in large organizations that may have multiple divisions conducting similar processes. For example, in large software development and manufacturing companies, a firm may have the same process if software development or production occurs at various locations or factories. This is necessary, as the capacity of one factory will not be enough to fulfill the needs. Hence, the performance of a process in Factory A can be benchmarked against its performance in Factory B. Benchmarking internally helps organizations compare processes with each other to get a better sense of relative strengths and weaknesses of an individual process. The benefit of internal benchmarking is the convenience and the ease of information availability. The limitation is that if all processes are doing equally badly, organizations may not be aware of this, as they are comparing bad with bad. Hence, internal benchmarking is almost always used in conjunction with external benchmarking reference points such as competitors, industry or processes.

Competitor benchmarking, as the name implies, involves comparing an organization's processes relative to its competitors. This is an ideal approach in highly competitive sectors where a company must always outperform its competitors to survive in the marketplace. If a competitor is doing a process better than your organization you have reason to be concerned, as it is a sign of a potential threat to your process. Most organizations will not have a hard time identifying their competitors; however, the challenge is to get hold of competitor information on their processes, which may not be easy to come by.

While getting information on specific competitors may be difficult, it may be easier to get hold of industry-level information at an aggregate level. Comparing processes to the industry gives organizations a sense of how they are doing when compared to the industry averages. This helps them identify whether they are doing better or worse than the average. If they are doing better than the average, they may want to see how they can do even better. Alternatively, if they are doing worse than the industry average, they have serious opportunities to improve their processes by figuring out what the other organizations are doing that they are not, and they also face serious threats of becoming laggards in the industry if they do not change and improve their processes.

Finally, organizations can compare their processes to other processes across industries. For instance, if they are in the management consulting business they can compare the performance of their accounts receivable function not only with other such functions within the management consulting industry, but also with firms that may be in the sectors of sales and retail, healthcare, insurance, etc. Their goal here is to identify best practices across the wide range of organizations that conduct a given process. They are looking at what they can learn from processes that are conducted both within and outside their industry. The benefit of conducting such a benchmarking is that organizations may deduce opportunities to improve their processes from practices found outside their industry.

Once you benchmark your organization's process you will be able to devise an appropriate SLA. Your SLA should be realistic and hence should reflect acceptable measures of success. Benchmarking helps you identify these levels of services. For instance, if a competitor who is the leader in accounts collection is able to turn over its accounts receivable within X days, you should feel confident that if you improve your processes you can also achieve this goal. Benchmarking enables you to devise the indicators of what you would like to expect from the outsourcing engagement in terms of results and service performance.

Outsourcing strategies

Before defining the needs of the project, you must do three things. First, you must decide the boundaries of the outsourcing project. This involves deciding what is to be included in the outsourcing project and what is outside its bounds. Second, you have to be clear on whether you want to conduct the outsourcing effort as one project or multiple projects. Third, you may want to, for the last time, examine whether outsourcing is your preferred strategy or whether you can solicit internal bids for the work and move the process from one location to another. These three issues are critical decisions as they will play a vital role in determining the level, scope and effort required for the outsourcing project (see Figure 4.1).

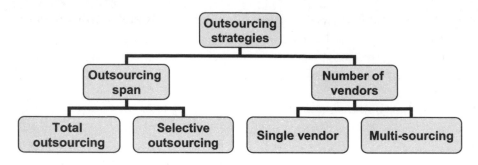

Figure 4.1 Outsourcing strategies

Total outsourcing versus selective outsourcing

Total outsourcing typically involves transferring more than 80 per cent of the function to a vendor. Total outsourcing mainly deals with functional or competency outsourcing and goes beyond simple individual outsourcing. These projects are usually complex and risky. Moreover, they are long-term projects due to the amount of work needed to be outsourced and hence reap benefits only in the long term and not the short term. Total outsourcing can cause major technological and business strategy limitations if you lack the clear understanding of magnitude and scope at the time the contract is signed. Failure can be very costly. Total outsourcing should only be pursued by organizations that have had experience with smaller outsourcing projects. Jumping into a total outsourcing effort without adequate experience can be disastrous, as one will lack an effective and efficient process to follow. Moreover, in case of failure, the organization could be crippled instantaneously, due to the magnitude of the work.

The alternative to total outsourcing is selective outsourcing. This is where the organization outsources smaller segments of a function. Selective outsourcing, however, is not a panacea. An organization should be extremely careful in demarking which segments are going to be outsourced. As discussed in the section above, the organization should be clear on the interdependencies between processes and how these are going to be managed. It should take a systemic view of the business and in doing so it should ensure that processes being outsourced can be integrated back into the organization without serious disruptions. Moreover, the organization needs to account for the fact that in the future some other segments may be candidates for outsourcing and hence it must be able to integrate the current outsourced work with future outsourcing plans.

Single vendor or multi-sourcing?

Going with a single vendor for the outsourcing project has some interesting benefits. First, you have only one party to deal with. One person is responsible for the effort and for ensuring that the effort is executed with rigor and clarity. There are fewer overheads in terms of managing when dealing with one vendor. However, there are some risks. Relying on one vendor exposes an organization to risks in case the vendor fails to deliver, as it is 'putting all its eggs in one basket'. Moreover, relying on one vendor can lock your organization into the vendor, as the latter will have knowledge about your business and the initial cost of getting a vendor up to speed with the business knowledge is substantial enough to deter you from investing the time and effort needed to indoctrinate new vendors about the intricacies of your business. We can term this 'the lock-in effect'. If you are using one vendor for your processes for an extended period, the cost of switching over to a new vendor will be expensive, as the new vendor will require greater resources to learn about your business and then to provide the appropriate services. Hence, at the end of the contract you may just continue with the same incompetent vendor, as there is a high cost to be paid to get another one involved with the business. Going with one vendor is an ideal strategy to employ if the project you are sourcing is hard to decompose into components that can be worked on independently by multiple parties. The map of process dependencies should give you a good idea on how tightly coupled the various processes are.

Multi-sourcing is when you outsource functions to more than one vendor. Multi-sourcing involves breaking up the project into several components that can be handled by independent vendors and usually occurs during a total outsourcing project. Multi-sourcing encourages competition between vendors and creates a shared objective to perform at high levels. This is because vendors fear losing the business to another vendor. It also balances your risk because you are not 'putting all your eggs in one basket'. If one vendor is not performing, you can move services to another vendor that is already involved. Multi-sourcing often results in more competitive bids from multiple vendors than from a single provider. Moreover, multi-sourcing efforts are ideal when the item being outsourced is of a sensitive nature. Most defense departments usually engage in multi-sourcing efforts for projects that are highly sensitive. The defense departments have the knowledge about the overall system being outsourced and then decompose the overall system requirements into a series of individual components. Vendors are then solicited to work on each component independently, thus preventing them from knowing about the overall architecture of the system. Moreover, in case there are any security breaches to one of the vendor's systems, the extent of the damage will be limited to one component rather than the overall system.

Multi-sourcing agreements can only be employed when you are able to break your processes into independent parts that can be worked on by different parties. Multi-sourcing may be an option if you have several high-quality vendors who are candidates for a given project and would like to get each one's expertise to contribute to a distinct component of the overall process. For instance, it is common to find such arrangements in large information systems outsourcing projects where multiple vendors collaborate to complete the project, each one bringing his or her unique expertise to bear on the project.

Multi-sourcing isn't for everybody, though. It can be a nightmare to manage, unless you have processes and procedures to establish and manage multi-vendor relationships. In a multi-sourcing agreement the organization has the burden of integrating the various work components of the various vendors and then piecing them together. Hence, to be able to successfully maneuver multi-sourcing initiatives, the organization must be good at integration efforts and have a background in outsourcing engagements.

In-source or outsource?

For a final time you need to check that you are sure that you are going to outsource the process. The reason you need to revisit this decision here is simple – internal benchmarking, as discussed above, may reveal some interesting information. If you find out that there are other locations within your organization – such as other departments, teams or foreign locations – that are exceeding expectations in terms of performance when compared to the process you are planning to outsource, it may be a good idea to think about sourcing the work to these areas.

In-sourcing of work, a form of moving work from one location to another, is ideal if benchmarking reveals that there are areas within your organization that are excellent in conducting a process, both when compared to other areas within your organization and also in comparison to external parties such as your competitors, industry averages or information from process benchmarking. Many organizations make the mistake of overlooking the process of internal bidding of work. If there are areas within your organization that are capable of doing the work at your desired service levels, why not allow these areas to bid on the project and conduct the work? There are several distinct advantages to keeping the work in-house. For one, you do not have to spend a lot of effort introducing the vendor to the details of your organization. Second, you do not have to deal with integrating different organizational cultures. Third, you will have little work to do in terms of negotiation and contracting as the work is conducted in-house. And finally, retaining the work in-house allows you to reduce the overall disruption in the organization.

In-sourcing is only good if you are sure that there are competent areas willing to do the work and meet the desired service levels. In-sourcing should not be done if you are trying to cut costs or want to abandon the process of moving through the outsourcing life cycle. Also, in-sourcing will not be a good idea for an organization where internal politics are severe. These organizations are characterized by executives who strive to gather support for their initiatives at the expense of the overall good of the organization. For example, meeting regional sales goals is more important for a regional manager than sharing leads and sales tactics with other executives so that the overall sales of the organization can be improved. These organizations will not have the right climate to move work from one location or sector to another, as this would signify that one executive is losing power while another is gaining it. Ego clashes will affect the well-intentioned process of in-sourcing. Outsourcing to an external party will be advisable here, as this will not be internally disruptive.

Defining the needs

Having done all the background work, you are now ready to define the needs of the process. Defining the needs for an outsourcing project is no different from defining the needs of any other project. Hence, we will not go in-depth into the well-understood practices of good requirements definition. Instead, we will pay attention to the two main dossiers that need to be prepared during the needs-analysis process.

The two main deliverables of the needs-analysis effort are the statement of work (SOW) and the request for proposals (RFP). One might think of the two documents in terms of how organizations advertise for employment positions. The RFP can be thought of as the job description that is posted on the internet or in the classified section of the newspaper. It states, at a high-level, the position your organization is looking to fill, the requirements of the work, the characteristics of the ideal candidate and a general and enticing description of your organization that should motivate potential candidates to apply for the job. The SOW, on the other hand, is the detailed requirements for the work. This is normally the statement or argument that led to the creation of the job position advertisement. It clearly defines the nature of the work to be performed, what the expected tasks are and how they should be conducted, how the work fits into the overall business strategy and other efforts being undertaken. It is these details that are used to decide whether the person interviewing for the job should be hired or not. Both the job description and the details of the job position, like the RFP and the SOW, are intermittently linked and connected; one feeds off the other. Since the SOW is the more detailed of the two, we will cover this first.

The SOW

The SOW must clearly define the work to be done and its boundaries. It must also specify the milestones and time frames, expected end product or results and criteria for evaluating performance and quality. The SOW is more defined and specific in terms of the outsourcing project than the RFP and should cover the four items described below.

Components of the SOW

Scope of the project
Details of the work assignment
SLAs
Roles and responsibilities

Scope of the project

A clear description of the scope of the project or service to be outsourced is a critical component of the SOW. Writing a description involves listing the services to be outsourced and their features and functionalities. It is important to be comprehensive in the descriptions, as these will be used by the vendors to price the outsourcing project and also for evaluation by vendors in terms of whether they have the necessary resources and expertise to conduct the work.

No service or project exists in isolation; hence, to provide the vendor with a clear sense of the work being outsourced, it is pivotal that you provide some background information. The background information should include an overview of how the work being outsourced fits in the big picture of the organization.

Details of the work assignment

The SOW needs to outline the details of how the work being outsourced should be performed. This involves detailing the specifications and requirements of the work and clearly stating any standards to expected workflow models that need to be followed. In software engineering, for example, there are many options one can follow in terms of a system-development methodology. If the organization has a preferred approach, this needs to be identified. Requirements such as the quality control measures and checks also need to be covered here. For instance, in the case of a software project, the SOW should detail how the software would be tested, how defects would be recorded, analyzed and corrected, and how each version of the software would be evaluated.

You need to be very detailed here in covering all aspects of the work. Leaving anything out is dangerous, as that will allow for ambiguity in terms of how the vendor does the work. The rule to follow here is one of materiality: if there is something important that affects how the work should be done, it should be material enough to document in the SOW. Hence, while you would not specify that you would like all documents to be prepared in single- or double-spaced format, you would probably need to document that testing of the system or work being outsourced needs to be conducted by a joint team representing both the vendor and client organizations.

The SLA

The SOW needs to clearly state what you expect in terms of the SLA. The SLA should be clearly stated, easy to understand, easy to measure and based on your thorough benchmarking analysis. A common mistake made by organizations is to have ambiguous and incoherent SLAs that cannot be measured objectively. This makes them very difficult to implement and hence just useless. It is always a good idea to state the exact methods of computation for measuring the SLA so as to be clear. For instance, if an organization has an SLA that relates to the downtime of a system, it should be able to precisely state how its expects this downtime to be calculated – per month, per week or per day. Moreover, it needs to state clearly what is considered downtime – is downtime counted for a system that is partially available? The answer would depend on the kind of system. The point is that these specifics need to be clearly stated so that they can be measured and evaluated.

Another error is to have one SLA too many. These agreements should be used to measure the most important items about processes that concern your outsourcing project, and not to measure just about everything.

Roles and responsibilities

Finally, the SOW needs to state the roles and responsibilities of the client and vendor organizations, ie who does what and when. Having a clear assignment of roles and responsibilities up front prevents finger pointing later on in the evaluation of the outsourcing relationship. For each role and responsibility, it is not sufficient just to identify it as being conducted by the vendor or client; the SOW must be more specific than that. Actual position names such as 'business manager' or 'quality assurance analyst' need to be specified. Doing so results in specifics that hold each organization accountable.

Five characteristics of a good SOW

1. Unambiguous
2. Complete
3. Consistent
4. Containing metrics that are clear, very easy to measure and comprehensive
5. Traceability

Characteristics of a good SOW

The SOW for a software project will differ from the SOW for a project involving the outsourcing of a human resource function. However, a good SOW is absolutely essential to the success of outsourcing efforts. We have witnessed many outsourcing failures arising from poorly calibrated SOWs. A well-crafted SOW will have several characteristics.

A good SOW will be unambiguous. Two people reading the SOW should come to the same conclusions as to what the outsourcing work involves. Having an ambiguous SOW is a sure way to start a futile outsourcing relationship. We recommend that representatives from each functional area of the organization read, analyze and interpret the document. Doing so will help the organization get multiple perspectives on the SOW, capture ambiguities and address them. The SOW is the foundation document, akin to a blueprint for constructing a house, on which the outsourcing work is based. Just imagine what it would be like to construct a building or house with ambiguous interpretations of a blueprint!

The SOW must be complete. While unambiguity ensures clarity, completeness is important for the SOW to reflect the complete project. Going back to the analogy of the blueprint for a house, for suppliers actually to construct the house the blueprint must include details from the foundation to the roof and from one wall to another. In terms of the SOW, the organization must be sure to include the details of all processes and also the connections between processes. Work concerning each process must be clearly specified and also the interconnections between processes must be detailed. Having an incomplete SOW will lead to incomplete outsourcing contracts and poor relationships with the vendors. This is because you will have to renegotiate a contract with the vendor to include items that were left out from the original SOW, most often being at the vendor's mercy, which normally results in an increase in the original cost of the outsourcing project. A good SOW will also include a brief description of the business justification for each work task, ie the rationale for conducting the task.

Consistency is also important. We have seen several SOWs that are complete and unambiguous, but are inconsistent in their terminology. In the use of scales and metrics, for example, consistency is paramount. For example, use of the English system or the metric system needs to be consistent. If work hours are evaluated based on a 40-hour work week, this needs to be consistent throughout the SOW. Having inconsistencies will lead to conflicts in interpretations and to poor calculations.

The SOW should include metrics against which the outsourcing project will be judged. These metrics should be clear, very easy to measure and verify and be comprehensive, to include key objectives of all stakeholders of the outsourcing project. Clear metrics are normally the best metrics. Having metrics that are ambiguous and difficult to calculate is normally equivalent to having no metrics at all. Metrics should also be fair. In terms of fairness, an organization should be up front about having metrics that evaluate how well it, as the client, is performing in the relationship, in addition to metrics that evaluate the vendor. The client must also be clear in identifying who will be responsible for evaluating the metric, whether this is a specific group in the organization or a specific person, and how deviations from the expected performance should be discussed and resolved.

The final SOW is normally the outcome of several iterations of debates, discussions, revisions and negotiations. These normally occur as the SOW is created, so the final version of the SOW could be version 200 of the originally calibrated SOW. It is, therefore, important for the internal purposes of the organization that changes made through iterations of the SOW be captured and documented to enable traceability. The organization will be able to track the history of the current requirements and examine how they have evolved over time and, more important, understand why. Tracing the evolution of each SOW will be much easier if you are clean and precise in documentation. This would involve giving each requirement a specific ID number, categorizing requirements by type (such as whether they are core or auxiliary), capturing the source of the requirement (ie who was responsible for bringing it up and including it in the original SOW), capturing dependencies (ie how the requirement effects others), capturing conflicts and capturing changes. Capturing conflicts is important, because in the early stages of writing a SOW you may actually have two or more requirements that are in conflict with one another so that meeting one requirement will adversely affect another. Over time, we would hope that such conflicts would be eliminated. Capturing changes includes data that has been modified, dates of the modification, rationale for the change and source of the change.

Having the ability to go back and trace the evolution of a SOW will be critical if members of the original outsourcing planning team leave and new members have to be brought on board. The new members can look at the history and get up to speed on what has transpired. Moreover, in cases where the outsourcing efforts are successful (or fail) the history of the SOW can be evaluated to see what key issues in the requirements definition stage may have contributed to the outcome, and where.

The SOW represents the details of the outsourcing efforts and must be clearly written and complete. It is the foundation on which the outsourcing effort will be based. A high-level description of the SOW makes its way into an RFP.

Components of the RFP

1. Sourcing requirements and scope
2. The vendor
3. Process and quality issues
4. The client – corporate profile

The RFP

The RFP contains four major sections: sourcing requirements and scope, the vendor, process and quality issues and a corporate profile of your organization.

Sourcing requirements and scope

This section will be a high-level description of the SOW. Your goal here is to clearly define the main process that you seek to outsource and its environmental details. The major component of this section includes a clear description of problems, current issues and the areas that you would like to improve, the expected benefits that you plan to reap from outsourcing, the service level that you expect from the vendor with a high-level description of the vendor evaluation process and the ideal characteristics you are looking for in the vendor in terms of experience, knowledge and capability. As an analogy, think about a job advertisement – you cannot expect to outline every peculiarity of the position you seek to hire for in the advertised job description, but must focus on clearly specifying the high-level details.

The vendor

The vendor section must clearly state the vendor value proposition, practices and demographics you are looking for. This section must answer two key questions:

- What kind of vendor would be the ideal candidate to form a partner?
- What do you expect in terms of knowledge, value propositions and practices from such a vendor?

To answer the first question, you must be clear on several items: first the demographic details of the vendor. These will include details such as whether you are seeking a vendor that is onshore, offshore or near-shore, years it has been in business, projects experience and expertise, available infrastructure and the capabilities and strengths that meet your requirements. An ideal answer to the first question should help a vendor decide if it is the right candidate even to consider answering the RFP. Hence, you must be specific in defining the demographics of the ideal vendor. For example, if you state that you are seeking a vendor who has global experience, chances are that you are going to get responses from a wide-ranging group of service providers. However, if you specify that you are seeking vendors who have expertise in the Far East or the Middle East, you will have narrowed down the pool considerably.

In addition to stating the demographic details of the ideal vendor, you must be clear on stating the practices you expect the vendor to have in place. For example, if you expect the vendor to meet ISO quality standards or practice six-sigma quality methodologies, these must be explicitly stated. If you expect the vendor's processes to be compliant to certain standards, these must also be specified. In the case of software projects, organizations very often look for vendors who have reached level 4 or 5 on the Capability Maturity Model (CMM). When entering into alliances with vendors in offshore locations, you may want to go with organizations that have branches in the country where your organization is located or that are registered with the commerce authorities in their countries. You may also want to state the kind of accounting and costing standards you expect the vendor to follow, so that when pricing or other issues arise, they can be shared with common understanding.

Process and quality issues

The section on process and quality issues draws from the SOW and clearly states the expectations in terms of the work to be conducted. Here, only the most severe and critical issues of the work project are stated. These would include details such as the kind of disaster recovery and backup capabilities expected of the vendor, the kind of security practices that you would need to feel comfortable about before outsourcing the work, the kind of relationship management process you would like to have, the nature of metrics and how the outsourcing work would be evaluated, the kind of approach you would take to work with the vendor and how the vendor would work with you to get the project completed.

The client – corporate profile

The final section of the RFP will provide a clear description of the client organization. It should describe your goals, missions and value statements, the kind of business you are in and your expectations in terms of business partners. It should state the kind of markets you target and are involved with, the industry verticals you focus on and the markets you plan to enter. It should encapsulate the current strategy of the business and the expected enhancements to the strategy in the near future. For example, in the case of a marketing company that has focused on operations in North America and in the electronics industry and is planning to expand its reach to the Middle East or South American markets, clearly outlining such information can result in executives finding a vendor that appreciates the rate of growth they expect and can scale up to their future needs.

Finally, this section must clearly state what you value about your business and what is most important to you in terms of a vendor. For example, you must specify whether you want a vendor that is stable and has a well-defined infrastructure or one that is constantly innovating and dynamic.

The RFP process is obviously a major step in selecting a vendor. Before sending an RFP, your vendor evaluation and selection team must meet to ensure a common understanding of the evaluation criteria, selection process and the scoring system. Only then can you ensure that confidentiality, accountability and objectivity will be maintained throughout the RFP process. Document your vendor evaluation and selection process in the RFP and follow that process to maintain fairness and objectivity. You also should designate a single point of contact from your company to address all vendor inquiries. The RFP must include an executive summary including an understanding of the scope, objectives, priorities, strategies and requirements. The proposal must identify critical success factors for the outsourcing initiatives from the vendor's perspective.

Some of the criteria to ask the vendor organization to contribute in its response to the RFP include the experience and skill levels of its staff, background and experience in your industry, the SLA it is expected to meet; its staffing plan and its cost control plan. You must draft an RFP that gets the following items sent to you in the vendor response: a company profile including principal owners and the company's principal business, corporate goals, office location and service centers, financial statement reflecting stability and capability and previous experience related to the requirements of the RFP. The vendor should demonstrate existing technical and management expertise within its organization and include a response to each of the minimum qualifications identified in the RFP.

Conclusion and checklist

In this chapter we have discussed how to conduct the needs-analysis process. In the next chapter, we take on the task of detailing how to evaluate the RFP responses from the vendors. Defining the needs of an organization can be a daunting task, requiring a huge commitment by the client organization. Many organizations struggle to define their overall needs and objectively identify their core competencies. If you do not possess the internal expertise that can be brought to bear to write up good requirements, it is wise to seek outside counsel. Writing up requirements involves effort and expertise. We do not cover the process of requirements gathering in this book, not because it is not important, but because it is common to any project management effort. It is important for companies to identify viable outsourcing process candidates, the appropriate outsourcing business model and to document clearly RFP and SOW requirements. Companies must be prepared to commit the appropriate cross-functional resources required to conduct the ever-so-important due diligence required during this outsourcing life-cycle phase. In our experience, companies that short-change the process will uncover numerous issues later down the line that can hinder or even cripple the outsourcing initiative. Again, there is no substitute for investing the time, people and money required to define your needs. Do not leave it up to your vendor to define your needs. That's a high stake game you cannot afford to lose.

The following key questions will serve as a checklist that you have effectively defined the needs of the outsourcing project.

- Do you understand the process you are going to outsource?
- Have you mapped out the process dependencies?
- Is there a business-value argument for outsourcing the process?
- Have you checked constraints on the process that would restrict your ability to outsource it?
- Have you conducted a thorough benchmarking analysis?
- Have you chosen between total or selective outsourcing?
- Have you chosen between going with a single vendor or multiple vendors?
- Have you considered the potential of in-sourcing the work?
- Do you have internal expertise to conduct the requirements-gathering process?
- Have you crafted a thorough SOW?
- Have you crafted a thorough RFP?

5 Vendor assessment

There is an interesting analogy to the various stages of the outsourcing life cycle we have discussed so far. We can think of the outsourcing process as similar to how people make friends or find lifelong partners. Without an adequate sense of his or her needs, it will be very difficult for an individual to enter and sustain a successful relationship. As a first step, the individual must ask, 'Am I ready for a relationship?' This is hardly a trivial question. The answer will depend on the individual's current situation, goals and aspirations, lifestyle, time, resources, etc. Unless a person seriously contemplates this question, there is a risk of entering into the wrong type of relationship or entering into a relationship with the wrong kind of individual. In certain situations an individual may poorly estimate the need for a relationship and hence remain in seclusion erroneously. All these outcomes are undesirable.

Once an individual decides that there is a justified need for a relationship, the next step is to seek out the right type of relationship and partner. It is important to differentiate between the right *relationship* and the right *partner*. Relationship types can vary from finding a pen pal, making acquaintances or friends, to seeking a soul mate. Each relationship has its associated set of benefits and costs – conceivably, the effort needed to sustain friendships will be lower than courting a soul mate. This was the topic of discussion in the previous chapter where we focused on ensuring that the organization clearly specified the needs of the outsourcing project and how to formulate a statement of those needs. Through the RFP and SOW organizations clearly state their needs and requirements and solicit bids from vendors who are ready to meet the needs. Most often, after sending out an RFP an organization will be inundated with more information and more bids from vendors than it imagined. This chapter focuses on the challenge of conducting a thorough vendor assessment to pick out the right business partner to meet your needs.

After identifying the type of relationship, an organization is ready to begin the search for the right partner, ideally one who meets its individual needs and is willing to engage in the relationship of its choice. This ideal, as anyone experienced in forging relationships will tell you, is not always realistic. The partner you want may not want to engage in the relationship of your choice or you may not find the right partner to meet the peculiarities of the relationship you want. To ensure a good match, organizations must engage in a process of getting to know the partner and begin dialogue. Negotiations normally occur during the initial courtship phase. Failure to reach appropriate compromises could lead to early termination of the relationship. If an agreement is reached, the relationship begins 'officially'. This could be signified by the signing of a contract, as in the case of a marriage, or a handshake or similar formal gestures.

In this chapter we will discuss how to go about choosing the right vendor to meet your needs. In the next chapter we will examine the issues involved in negotiating and contracting. The following chapters discuss issues involved in starting and managing the relationship, along with the issues of continuance, modification or termination of the relationship.

An important point that we need to reiterate from Chapter 2 on the outsourcing life cycle is that vendor assessment should be handled independently by the organization, without *any* undue influence from external vendors. We advise against going out and talking to or interacting with vendors in any kind of depth and detail without first completing an independent vendor assessment. The reasoning is quite simple; most vendors will want you to get in touch with them. Once a connection is made, they most likely have pre-planned sales pitches, fancy slide shows and other bells and whistles to dazzle you with. If you do not carry out a thorough vendor assessment independently by evaluating responses to the RFP and SOW before going into a discussion or negotiation with the vendor, you will not be able to separate the real information from the misinformation or 'myth-information'.

Conversely, if you have done a good vendor assessment you will be advantageously positioned to be successful in negotiation and contracting. Interacting with vendors should only be conducted after the organization has been able independently to assess information about the vendor.

We will begin our discussion by highlighting the different kinds of vendor an organization can have. Next, we will describe the response to the RFP. It is important for the organization to identify the key components of an RFP response, so as to differentiate completed and thorough responses from those that are less prepared. Following this, we will discuss the step-by-step process of evaluating vendors. We conclude the chapter by looking at common errors made during vendor selection.

Types of vendor

Vendors can be classified on a number of dimensions ranging from the geographical proximity (such as onshore, near-shore or offshore), to their size (small, small-to-medium, medium-to-large, large). There are also vendors that specialize in process work and those that focus more on project work. These classifications affect the nature of the type of outsourcing relationship and have been addressed in the Introduction. In this section, we would like to highlight the two salient dimensions on which to classify vendors in order to conduct a thorough vendor assessment: vendor expertise and vendor resources (see Figure 5.1).

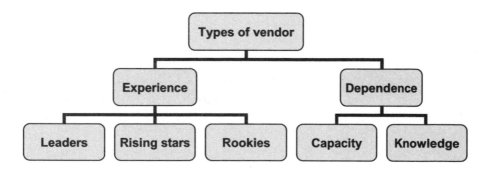

Figure 5.1 Types of vendor

Leaders, rising stars and rookies

Vendors can differ in how much expertise they have in the given domain of outsourcing – leaders, rising stars and rookies. In the case of software development outsourcing efforts, countries like India, Ireland and Canada have clearly established themselves as leaders in the field. Organizations involved in outsourcing efforts in these countries, for example Infosys, TCS, Wipro and Cognizant, have some of the most mature software development processes and consistently rank among the most profitable software organizations. Compared to these, China, Mexico, Brazil, South Africa, Poland, Russia, Hungary, Singapore, Malaysia and even the Czech Republic are the rising stars of software development. These countries have put in place the necessary infrastructure, such as telecommunications, and also are building a budding workforce that is highly trained and knowledgeable in areas of software development. Finally, there are organizations in countries like Thailand, Vietnam, New Zealand, Bulgaria, Ukraine, Costa Rica, Argentina and Chile that are rookies in terms of software development. These countries have made a conscious decision to support organizations that want to explore the software development market, but are yet to put in place all required and necessary infrastructures to help them compete successfully.

Needless to say, there are pros and cons to each type of vendor. If an organization chooses a leading organization it can, to a large degree, be sure of the quality of the vendor's service, reputation and credibility. However, these advantages carry costs. Leaders may not be willing to comprise much, as they are constantly sought after for business. Moreover, they may have large backlogs in terms of work assignments and potential future projects, so their interest and dedication to a new customer – unless the customer is highly significant and has long-term relationship possibilities – will be less than adequate. If an organization is considering outsourcing processes that are seen as core competencies, it should strive to partner with leaders in the industry. The risk of experimenting with rising stars or rookies will be much too high. Instead, it needs to find a business partner who has an established reputation in the area and is known to innovate, so that it can ensure access to superior knowledge.

If a firm chooses a rising star, it will find an organization that is willing to prove itself and hence will be eager to get the business.

Rising stars are good places to get a beta or test project started to see how things pan out. Shell, DHL and Motorola have already set up operations in Malaysia to complement some of the work they have with leader organizations. Rising stars could eventually overtake the current leaders, hence it is wise not to write them off completely. However, we would not advise sending highly mission-critical projects to these organizations, for the simple reason that they may not have the necessary maturity or experience to handle them. When choosing a rising star, a firm must make sure that it conducts a thorough background check of the organization and also checks current client references.

Rookies are interesting for a number of reasons, most of all because organizations have the least amount of information on them to make decisions; hence the risk factor is quite high. We know that an organization just entering the outsourcing vendor business faces stiff competition both from the leaders and the rising stars in the industry. Hence, it is likely that many of them will close down or be bought out by the more successful organizations. Yet, rookies can survive and may mature if they are nurtured and given a space. Our advice would be to seek out rookies who have forged alliances with some of the larger and more established outsourcing vendors. For example, companies in India who are leaders in software development have begun to open operations in some countries that are currently rookies or novices in the outsourcing world. Rookies can also be employed for low-volume and low-significance outsourcing projects, so that they can be tested. Under no circumstances do we recommend using rookies for the outsourcing of core competencies, no matter how much of a bargain you may get on the cost of the project.

Resource-based classification

The second classification to be concerned with is the type of vendor resources your organization would like to access. This requirement will be defined and decided when conducting the needs analysis. To recap from the previous chapter, you need to ask yourself what you are looking for in a vendor – is your dependence on capacity or on knowledge and expertise? If the former, you would not need a vendor who is a leader, as leaders normally are better suited for situations where you are looking for expertise. In terms of dependence on capacity, the conventional wisdom of going with the lowest cost vendor is normally correct. However, you must make sure that the vendor meets the requirements of background checks, risk assessments and other details that we will discuss later in the chapter. To cite an example, if an organization is looking to outsource human resource functions, it is probably searching for a vendor who has the requisite human resource management knowledge to be able to carry out its human resource work. However, it should also be able to ensure that the vendor has the necessary infrastructure to deal with the required number of transactions (in this case, transactions per employee). The point is that dependence on capacity and knowledge are not mutually exclusive and must be taken into account in an integrated manner. It is important, however, that you have a clear idea which factor plays a critical role. If you are seeking dependence on knowledge, this should be your primary criterion for selecting vendors, rather than searching for vendors who have capacity capabilities, and vice versa.

Response to the RFP and SOW

While no two responses to the RFP and SOW will be the same, there are certain common elements that should be present in any response. Upon receipt of the response, you must evaluate it for its completeness, detail and comprehensiveness. A vendor that does not take due diligence in preparing a response should be eliminated from the vendor assessment process as this shows clear lack of interest or respect for your business.

Components of the response to the RFP and SOW

Cover page
Title page
Executive summary
Vendor profile
Engagement details
Cost estimates
Client references

A response statement should be viewed as your first impression of the vendor and must be evaluated as such. The response statement should contain the following key items:

- Cover page signed by the authorized vendor representative.
- Title page. This should include a brief vendor introduction statement, a statement that acknowledges that the vendor is responsible for all acts, omissions and errors in the response, contact information where questions and issues regarding the responses can be made and, finally, contact information of key vendor personnel who will be responsible for the negotiation process.
- Executive summary. This should include a demonstration of the fact that the vendor clearly understands the scope, objectives, priorities, strategies and requirements presented in the RFP. It should also include rationale or argument that states why the vendor will be the best candidate for the job, an outline of critical success factors for the outsourcing initiative from the vendor's perspective, a high-level description of how the vendor proposes to work with the client during the outsourcing initiative and a statement of sponsorship from the vendor's executive level demonstrating support and commitment to the effort.
- Vendor profile. This should provide a detailed corporate profile by covering items such as: the company's mission, objectives, value statements, biographies of key executives and owners, locations of the headquarters and other principal locations and summary of financial indicators demonstrating the vendor's financial stability and capability. In addition, the vendor must provide information on its experience in handling similar work in the past, such as previous experiences relevant to the RFP, description of superior technical and management practices in the organizations that will help in carrying out the outsourcing work and a clear response to the minimum vendor qualifications stated in the RFP.
- Engagement details. This should include the intricacies of the proposed RFP by responding to all issues and requirements contained in the RFP. This normally entails: responding to the outsourcing objectives, contract priorities, the flexibility of the contract, stating any competing priorities that the vendor may

have, nature and approach of providing services, the vendor's management practices in the areas of contract management, strategic and operational planning, project planning and management training, staffing plans, performance measurement standards and intellectual property protection practices.

- Cost estimates. The vendor should clearly state the estimated cost of doing the work and clearly explain how the cost figure was arrived at. In cases where the vendor thinks that cost estimates may be incorrect, as the vendor is using incomplete information to compile the estimate, this must be stated. The vendor must also state the rationale for major line items in the costing plan.
- Client references. The vendor must provide references of its current or very recent clients. The references should detail contact information on personnel at the executive level who can discuss and provide information on the vendor's engagement. The statement on client references should also briefly describe the nature of the work and relationship with the referable organizations.

Not all responses will have the items highlighted above in the same order or within the same sections, but all responses should cover all elements discussed above. Failure on the part of the vendor to prepare a thorough response to an RFP shows immaturity, lack of preparation, or worse, lack of due care and consideration about the business opportunity, all of which should raise red flags in terms of considering the vendor. Sometimes responses received from vendors may have all the components discussed above, yet do not seem to answer any of the specific issues raised in the RFP or SOW. These responses must not be entertained, as they are probably standard responses that vendors have created to respond to any RFP or SOW. Vendors who do not prepare an adequate response to an RFP should not be allowed to consume organizational resources in terms of the vendor assessment process.

The process of vendor assessment

The process of vendor assessment can be best described as one of filtering and sifting. Criteria are applied in turn to the initial large collection of potential vendors and the number of candidates is reduced. Finally you arrive at a manageable set with whom you would like to begin the costly process of negotiations. Then, it is hoped, you will hone in on the right one to sign a contract with. The number of criteria you may have to apply to choose the vendor will remain the same regardless of projects, though there might be differences in the intensity or the strictness with which you apply particular criteria, based on the peculiar nature of the project. For example, if you are evaluating an outsourcing vendor from those you currently work with, you may not have to do as much of a background check, as this was presumably done before signing the original contract with the vendor. Comparatively, evaluating a vendor from a pool of vendors you have not done business with would be a far more rigorous process. We will now outline the five steps in vendor assessment (see Figure 5.2).

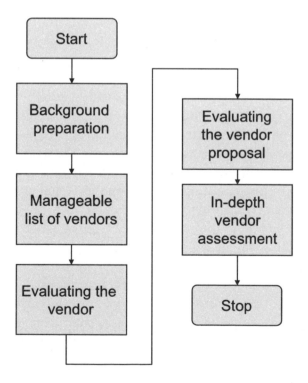

Figure 5.2 The vendor assessment process

1. Preparation

Preparation is needed before you can get started on evaluating vendors, to ensure that you have a solid and defined process in place to evaluate vendors. One of the first items to attend to is putting in place the vendor evaluation team, comprised of company representatives. This team should be cross-functional and must have members who have expertise in the core and auxiliary functions of the business, such as finance, legal, IT or production and operations. The team should understand its role and the process by which it will fulfill its goal of vendor evaluation. In order to do this, the team must go through an orientation or training program that clearly establishes a common understanding between the team members, outlines the vendor selection process, specifies the vendor scoring system and also clearly states the importance of objectivity and fairness in the vendor selection process.

Second, it is important to have a well-defined process in place to conduct the vendor evaluation. The process should ensure that the vendor evaluation is standardized, fair and documented. Having a standardized process is a must, as you will be required to compare vendors and cannot ensure a fair comparison if they have been evaluated on varying criteria or on different scoring methods. Fairness is important, and there should be as much transparency as possible in the selection process. Remember that a fair and equitable process is the best way to arrive at the right vendor, so making special accommodations for some vendors, putting up barriers for others and any other interventions will only result in the selection of the wrong vendor. The process should also allow you to capture information in a documented manner. In some organizations, there may be legal stipulations that may require an organization's vendor evaluation process to be subject to audit. For example, in the United States, government agencies have to be able to show fairness and equity in their allotment of private contracts. Governing bodies can, and in many cases do, require agencies to disclose their vendor selection process for auditing purposes. Hence, it is important that organizations document each stage, each decision and the associated rationale.

Third, you must allow sufficient time from the sending out of the RFP and SOW for vendors to respond. It will be futile to jump at the first responders and start the evaluation process. Actually, those who respond very quickly to an RFP should be suspect, as it takes time and effort to craft an adequate response. Allowing sufficient time will give all candidates an opportunity to compile and supply an adequate response.

2. Assembling a manageable list of candidates

In some instances, you may be inundated with responses to your RFP and the candidates need to be narrowed down to a manageable set to begin the process of choosing. Here, you are looking to apply broad or high-level criteria to reduce the pool of potential vendors. Many of these criteria can come from the work conducted in the needs-analysis stage. For example, if you decided to multi-source the project, you may want to weed out vendors who have broad knowledge but lack depth in any one component. In a multi-sourcing agreement, you are looking at assembling a group of vendors to work on multiple pieces of the project, so each vendor should have deep knowledge in the concept or component that they are working on. Other criteria could include the elimination of vendors by geographical location. If your plan is to go with a near-shore outsourcing vendor, offshore and onshore vendors can be eliminated. At the end of step 2, you have reduced the number of vendors to a set that you can focus on in greater depth.

3. Evaluating the vendors

The second seminal step is to begin evaluating the capability of each vendor in depth. Here you must create a list of desired attributes against which you measure each vendor, such as past dealing with the vendor, trust, brand name, references from current clients and areas of specialization. You also need to look at the capabilities and strengths of each vendor. This can be done by asking questions and talking to the vendors' current customers. Vendors should provide you with contacts from companies using their services. You should also look at each vendor's customer base. Are there vendors that resemble your organization in business and size? If so, their vendors should already be familiar with an evaluation process similar to yours. Other things to take into consideration include the vendors' business strategies, management practices and procedures, years of experience, types of certification and the award and reward mechanisms they use.

No matter what industry you are in, you need to look at key attributes when evaluating an outsourcing vendor. First, you need to know that the vendor can meet compliance standards for your industry. You also want to know whether the vendor can provide local support in the geographic area where the outsourcing work will take place. Look at the vendor's staffing practices and attrition rates. Ask for profiles of key employees such as managers, project leaders, senior developers and so on. You also want to know if the vendor has any pending or ongoing litigation with its customers. Other attributes you need to consider include the vendor organization's disaster recovery capabilities, how it will handle your data, its other physical and data security capabilities, its project management and relationship management procedures and the manner in which it manages change, problems, scalability and infrastructure. Again, look to see if the vendor has customers similar to yours and ask for current customer references.

What are the major considerations in selecting the right vendor for your outsourcing initiative? First, you need to be certain of the vendor's ability to meet its schedule and budget commitments. A good way to gauge this is through satisfaction levels of the vendor's current customers. You also have to look at the vendor's management philosophy and its past success with project management, including planning, tracking and control. Size and cost estimates are important here. Other things to look at include whether the vendor is working with any of your direct competitors. If so, there may be a conflict of interest.

You also have to look at technical issues. Does the vendor have the technical capability to meet the challenges of your project? Use your technical staff or independent parties to evaluate the vendor's product development capabilities. Take the vendor's vertical industry experience into account. Find out the vendor's quality methodologies. For example, in the case of software development projects, you may ask if they have Capability Maturity Model (CMM) certification and if they do, at what level. What metrics and performance practices does the vendor use? Answers to these issues will give you an indication of the rigor and clarity of the vendor's processes.

At this stage it is important that you have a thorough process in place to check vendors' backgrounds. This involves two steps. First, using the information the vendor provided about references, investigate the reference clients. This will help you validate the information provided by the vendor. Second, telephone each reference client and gather information on items such as performance of the work, satisfaction with the work, problem and dispute resolution process, transition plans, intellectual property issues and other pertinent matters. Promise confidentiality to the reference client, so that he or she may be frank and open in his or her evaluation of the vendor. Also, ask the reference client to both provide information on the vendor's performance independently and on the vendor's performance when compared to the reference client's past outsourcing relationships. It is always a good idea to have two or more people present when calling reference clients so that information documented from the interviews can be checked and validated.

In cases of discrepancy between the vendor-provided information and that gathered independently, you need to be wary of potential problems and negativities. Summarize the findings and share them with the vendor assessment team.

The above procedures are intended only as guidelines. You will have to arrive at your own criteria by looking at the needs of the project and the kind of vendor you are seeking. It is important, however, to follow some well-established rules when conducting the vendor assessment. First, apply the same set of criteria across all vendors. Do not bend the rules for any given vendor because then there will be no common baseline for comparison. Second, have at least three people with different backgrounds evaluate each vendor independently. This is to ensure that the vendor gets a thorough assessment. In the case of discrepancies in the reviewers' scores, have an open exchange of ideas and rationale. This will allow for a more thorough evaluation of the vendor. Third, when creating a list of attributes desired in a vendor, give them a ranking order, so as to grade the most important attributes in comparison to those that are not necessary but good to have. This will also help in evaluating the scores of vendor assessment and further reducing the list of vendors.

4. Evaluating the vendor's proposal

Once the vendors have been assessed it is time to evaluate each proposal. Here is where you look at the pricing issue. How much is the vendor's proposed price for the project and how does this meet with your expectations? Beware vendors that have priced the project significantly lower than the average. These vendors may be just trying to get your attention to call them for a negotiation session. Pricing should not be viewed as the decisive criterion. In addition to pricing, you must look at the details of each incoming proposal and evaluate it on the dimensions of completeness, clarity, detail and rigor. Completeness helps you to evaluate whether the vendor has been cognizant of all your needs and written a proposal with this in mind. Clarity is important as a demonstration of how easily the vendor is able to communicate with you on the areas of the proposal. Detail and rigor go hand in hand. For each requirement that you have set out, does the vendor demonstrate enough detail in its understanding of the issue and can you extrapolate some measure of rigor? Rigor helps you consider the quality issue. Do you feel comfortable enough to outsource the work to the vendor based on its demonstration of mastery of the steps required to complete the process?

A good best practice is to get a different set of scorers to evaluate each proposal, scorers other than those who evaluated the vendor, to rule out the possibility of bias or prejudgment. It may also be a good idea to 'blind' each proposal when sent to the scorer. In this way, the scorer will be making an assessment of the proposal without knowing who the vendor is.

Once the scores of both the vendor assessment and the proposal evaluations are in, you can further narrow down the list of vendors.

5. An in-depth look at the vendors

At this stage you take a closer look at the reduced list of vendors, with a focus on assessing their vulnerabilities. You must conduct a thorough risk assessment of each vendor. This would involve running through possible scenarios and asking what the main vulnerabilities of the vendor are. Is the vendor too focused on one client? If so, you could be in trouble if its major client pulls out its business, as this would threaten the vendor's survival. What about the political environment in which the vendor is based? For example, in the case of software development, given a choice between moving work to India or Pakistan, most would choose India because of its political stability, not to take anything away from their organizations' mature software processes. What about the financial assessment of the vendor? Does the vendor keep an adequate financial portfolio compared to other firms in its industry? Is the vendor successful in collecting its debts? These issues will give a sense of whether the vendor will come upon hard financial times in the immediate future. Are the vendor's current competitors coming up with newer innovations that have the potential to disrupt the current marketplace and affect the vendor? If so, you need to take this information into account when assigning a risk factor. These questions will give you a more thorough assessment of the vendor and, we hope, will help you narrow the list even further. The same guidelines discussed in step 3 apply for the risk assessment here and need to be followed.

When you have completed the above steps, you may be left with a pool of vendors with whom you can begin negotiations and discussions. It is important not to rush to negotiations before conducting the above steps. Negotiating is an expensive and time-consuming activity, so you want to be sure that the vendor you are negotiating with has the potential to be a business partner. Think of it in the context of making a decision about employing someone. You obviously would not want to interview every candidate from whom you receive a CV. You have to do a lot of up-front assessment before calling in a select pool of candidates for an interview and negotiations. The same principle is applicable here.

Six common errors when choosing vendors

1. Sacrificing needs analysis for a glamorous vendor
2. Evaluating a vendor with cost savings as the decisive factor
3. Poor risk assessment of the vendor
4. Rushing through the process of vendor selection
5. Lack of care in managing interactions between vendors
6. Failing to maintain a balance between using current and new vendors

---

Common errors when choosing vendors

Six common errors we have seen organizations make when conducting vendor assessment are discussed below.

1. Sacrificing the needs-analysis process for a glamorous vendor

There are many temptations to go with a brand-name outsourcing vendor. For instance, when organizations announce such an alliance to the market, the shareholders will normally respond positively, moving the stock price up. This is pleasing and gets good press. On the other hand, announcing a deal with a lesser-known vendor may not give organizations the same hype or praise. This kind of glamour is short-lived. After all, the market will keep a close eye on how well the alliance is doing throughout its duration. If the outsourcing alliance fails, it hardly matters whether the failure was with a brand-name vendor or with any no-name vendor. Actually, if you had an alliance with a brand-name vendor that failed, this bad news will be circulated more prominently in the business media. The point here is stay steadfast on your needs analysis. Do not get bullied or try to compromise on your needs just because of the urge to sign a deal. It is important to ensure that you get the best fit between the organizations to put a viable outsourcing relationship in place.

2. Evaluating a vendor with cost savings as the decisive factor

There is more to a relationship than just cost savings. You must look at the outsourcing relationship in the broader context of contributing to the organization's strategic advantages and adding value to the business. Cost savings are normally the most short-lived of the benefits of outsourcing, if the relationship is not a pleasant and fulfilling one. On the other hand, an organization can sustain cost savings and other competitive advantages in a viable outsourcing relationship. It is critical that an organization consider issues such as the vendor's competency, history, reputation and the risk-assessment factors when making the vendor assessment.

3. Poor risk assessment of the vendor

Incomplete risk assessment of the vendor could expose an organization to vulnerabilities. A vendor is a business partner and hence you must gather adequate knowledge about the vendor and its past dealings before deciding to engage in the business relationship. The first two common errors above and some of the material that follows (such as rushing through the vendor-selection process) have a dangerous outcome – incomplete risk assessment. Organizations are asking for trouble when they do not conduct vendor assessments with due diligence. In our opinion, it is better not to sign a deal and keep the work in-house, even if it is inefficient and costly, than to hand over work to a vendor that an organization does not completely assess. All vendors will bring some level of risk with them; this is a normal part of doing business. The challenge for the organization is to weigh the risk to decide what risks it is willing to bear and at what point the risk becomes greater than its set threshold. To go back to Chapter 3, this is why it is important to conduct the strategic assessment with particular focus on the risk-assessment process.

4. Rushing through the process of vendor selection

Do *not* rush through the process of vendor selection. As simple as this may sound, most organizations that we know do not follow this rule. Agreed, time is valuable, but taking the time to sift diligently through details and narrow down choices is time spent wisely and well. Rushing through the process will only result in choosing a vendor that is less than adequate. In some cases, the organization may find a brand-name vendor who has an established track record in the broad domain of outsourcing, say IT development. In appreciating the vendor's impressive track record, the client organization may relax its vendor-evaluation process of digging deeper and seeing which *areas* of 'IT development' the vendor is an expert in. Packaged software implementation? Customized application development? System integration? Not digging deeper will result in choosing a vendor who may be highly competent but in the wrong domain! In other cases, organizations may choose a vendor who does not have the necessary competency just because it was the first to submit a bid on the RFP when, ideally, they should be asking why the bid was submitted so quickly and if it was a standard bid used on just any RFP the vendor comes across!

5. Lack of care in managing interactions between vendors

When choosing vendors you must not overlook an important aspect – the cultural fit between the new vendor you plan on bringing in and your current list of vendors. Too often, this dimension is overlooked.

Most organizations will, rightfully, check to see if there is a cultural fit between the vendor organization and theirs. However, they forget to look at how the new vendor will work with the current vendors. This is a serious oversight, especially when organizations have projects that involve collaborations among different organizations. The ideal is a situation where there is both competition and collaboration between vendors – 'coopetition'! Organizations want each vendor to cooperate with the rest of the vendors so that the work can be completed in an effective and efficient manner. Yet they would also like to see a bit of friendly competition between vendors, in the sense that they want each of them to feel a sense of urgency in getting the work done. Healthy competition will improve the work performance of all parties involved in the project. An organization must realize this aspect as it goes about choosing vendors and must do everything possible to ensure that interactions between vendors are being managed appropriately. However, certain things should not happen – the organization, while promoting competition between vendors, should not show favoritism or pit one vendor against another. This behavior is childish and will come back to haunt the client organization, as vendors will realize what is happening and may choose to act in a way that will negatively impact the business relationship.

6. Failing to maintain a balance between using current and new vendors

In most cases, an organization has a choice to make: does it use its current vendors for the new outsourcing engagement or does it solicit inputs from a fresh set of vendors? This question will be explored in greater depth in the chapter on continuance, modification or exit strategies. For now, let us cover this question briefly. There is no easy answer to it, so all we can do is present the pros and cons of choosing either alternative. If you go with vendors who are already doing business with you, much of the process of vendor assessment becomes easier as you already have an established relationship with the vendor, and we hope it is positive, which is why you are considering extending the relationship. However, it may be this very familiarity that may result in your being blind to other novel, and possibly more viable, alternatives that exist in the market. If you go with a new vendor, there is a higher risk threshold, as you do not know as much. The vendor could perform miserably; on the other hand, the vendor could do an excellent job – you just do not know before the start of the outsourcing work. Our suggestion would be that, in most cases, if you have current vendors who have competencies in the areas of the new project and can perform the work with expected quality levels, do not take unnecessary risks and go with a new vendor. The bottom line is that it is just too costly to go through the life-cycle process of bringing a new vendor up to speed with the business and getting acclimatized to a new way of working. On the other hand, if you are considering terminating a relationship with an existing vendor or are witnessing downward trends in your current vendor list, because a vendor assumes it has 'locked' your future business, bringing in a new player might actually shake things up in a positive sense and provide a renewed sense of necessary but friendly competition among the vendors as they try to prove themselves.

Conclusion and checklist

In this chapter we have discussed how to go about choosing vendors. Vendor assessment is a phase not to be rushed through or conducted haphazardly. Remember, by conducting a vendor assessment you are in the process of choosing a business partner to whom you plan to open up your business. Your business partners and their vulnerabilities will have a bearing on your success and consequently can affect your failures.

Some companies have created vendor management offices (VMOs) to manage the interaction with vendors (Patton, 2005). These organizations have realized that it is better to centralize and control the interactions with vendors rather than have different units of the organization try to manage them. The VMOs oversee the evaluation of the responses to the RFP. They also monitor the performance of current vendors and in doing so can gauge which vendors are outperforming others and which ones should be candidates for contract terminations. The VMOs handle all negotiations with the vendors. Doing so allows them to channel all organizational requests through one venue, thereby giving the organization one voice. It also allows them to gain economies in negotiations, such as going after bulk discounts and bundling new services or requests with existing contracts. The VMOs also oversee the interactions between vendors in the context of multi-sourcing projects. The role of the VMO here is to ensure coordination of efforts between the various parties and also promote healthy competition between the vendors, so as to provide the organization with the best deal. The VMO makes sure that the vendors are aware that they are not the only option for the organization's business and that they must perform up to par or risk their contract being terminated.

Choosing the right vendor is an important and seminal step in the outsourcing process. Use the following questions as a checklist for vendor assessment:

● Do you have a representative vendor-assessment team?
● Is there a standardized, accepted and fair process for evaluating responses to your RFP and SOW?
● Have you devised high-level criteria to reduce the vendor list to a manageable set?
● Is there a process in place to conduct a background check for each vendor?
● Do you understand the criteria to apply when evaluating vendor proposals?
● Have you conducted the risk assessment for each vendor?
● Do you understand the common errors that occur when going through the vendor assessment? And do you have a plan to avoid these errors?

Now that you have chosen the right vendor, the next step is to ensure that you craft the right contract with the chosen organization. You now need to put on paper all your expectations and the vendor's promises – enter into the negotiation and contract phases.

6 Negotiation and contract management

In this chapter we outline how to put in place a working outsourcing relationship. This task normally involves two interrelated acts – negotiations and contract management.

Negotiations are a normal aspect of doing business, as organizations are all hoping to secure the best deal possible. Trying to strike a deal to secure an advantageous position for yourself is hardly unique to the outsourcing world. Negotiations are a part of almost any business deal. Have you ever purchased anything from a bazaar where bargaining was an option? If you did, and had poor negotiating skills, you probably overpaid – not a good outcome. However, think about going to purchase a commodity such as milk. Do you ever negotiate the price of a pint of milk or, for that matter, a pint of beer? No, it is simply not economical to do so, and what is more, it could get you thrown out of the store or pub. Similar dynamics occur when trying to negotiate an outsourcing relationship. Failure to appreciate the particularities of the relationship sought, the item being outsourced, the vendor's position and, more important, the position of the organization considering outsourcing, will almost always lead to a deal that is disadvantageous for one party or, in the worst cases, disadvantageous for both.

Negotiations normally have a finite time period, at the end of which they either end with an agreement or disagreement. In the latter case, one will negotiate with the next vendor of choice and hope for a better ending. In the case of the former, the next natural step is to codify the agreement in writing – contract management. In the contract management phase organizations codify all of the material discussed during the negotiations into a legal document that binds the vendor and client. The key operating premise is to put it in writing and sign on the dotted line. Without getting things in writing, ie in an explicit format, the chances are high that there will be abundant confusion between the vendor and client organization. Moreover, in case confusion does arise, how do they know which of the parties is right or wrong? Most of the time, the way disputes are resolved in a legal setting is through evaluation of the contract. The contract rules supersede any verbal agreements or discussions. If an agreement is not in writing, it is not accounted for in most cases. Moreover, if an item is important, it is best to get a commitment from the vendor in writing. We cannot understate the point that the contract represents the legal and most binding aspect of the outsourcing relationship.

The two acts of negotiation and contract management are closely interwoven. If you do not have good negotiation skills, it is highly likely that you will codify a contract that is not economically advantageous to you from the beginning. On the other hand, if you are excellent at negotiations, but fail to document the advantages secured via negotiations, the contract will not reflect these details, with the result that you will sign something other than what you asked for. We will explore the two acts of negotiation and contract management sequentially. We conclude the chapter by examining why outsourcing contracts are pivotal to the future of the outsourcing relationship.

Negotiation management

Any person has had an entire lifetime of negotiating experiences, some of which have had a positive ending, others less favorable. Most graduate business schools have entire courses on the topic of negotiation management, while any bookseller has more books on negotiation than one would care to read. Our intention here is not to go about explaining the art of negotiation management; rather, we will focus on those key aspects of negotiating an outsourcing contract that are often overlooked and underestimated. While some of these are applicable to any negotiation setting, a few are peculiar to getting involved in an outsourcing relationship. We will call our guidelines 'Ten essentials of good negotiation'.

Ten essentials of outsourcing negotiation

1. Know yourself
2. Know your vendor
3. Know your market
4. Prioritize your requirements
5. Know your time frame
6. Start from your position then move towards the vendor's
7. Have the right negotiation team
8. Appreciate cultural differences – organizational and national
9. Document, document, document
10. Negotiate towards a relationship not a contract

1. Know yourself

There is nothing that will kill a negotiation quicker than not knowing where one stands and what one's needs are. Unless an organization has a good understanding of where it stands, its needs and where it wants to be, negotiating will be difficult. Knowing yourself will call for being thorough in the stages of strategic assessment and needs analysis, as previously described. It is consequently of utmost importance that organizations do not scrimp on these stages or try to cut corners. Without a good understanding of their needs, no matter what happens at the negotiation table, a disastrous outcome is almost certain.

One element on being clear about your needs is making sure that all members of the negotiation team are on the same page. When negotiating with a vendor, there should be only one version of what the organization's needs are. Experienced vendors will know how to exploit disagreements between members of your negotiation team to their advantage. They will know how to play one against the other – the age-old 'divide and rule' policy. As an example, they may try to negotiate a term with one member of the team and then play on this agreement to get a buy-in from the rest of the team. To avoid scenarios such as this, it is absolutely essential that a united front be brought to the negotiation table.

2. Know your vendor

As discussed at length in the previous chapter, an organization must act with diligence in gathering information about its potential vendor. It is important to get a sense of what is going on in the background. No vendor, in our experience, will overtly discuss this background, especially when such information is negative and could adversely affect the signing of the contract. It is up to the client organization to do its best to get at such information, so as to have enough of a context to analyze the information, guarantees and promises made by the vendor during the negotiations. Each vendor has distinct areas of strengths and weaknesses that need to be analyzed thoroughly, both by examining each vendor individually and also by comparing them with each other.

Having adequate information about the vendors from the start will save an organization nightmares later in the outsourcing life cycle. To cite one example, one of us was involved in a vendor-assessment project where the unique expertise being brought to the table was that of competitive intelligence. During the course of work, it was discovered that some of the information provided by the vendor was faulty, what may be called small white lies. This set off alarm bells in a few heads. However, senior management did not want to give the vendor-assessment process more time and decided to ignore the misrepresentations as minor lapses. Lo and behold, the contract was signed, up-front payments as per the contract were made to the vendor and one week later the vendor announced bankruptcy. To make matters worse, the client organization was on the lowest priority of creditors claiming the assets of the company and recovered almost nothing of its payment. Situations like these waste not only the price paid up front for the contract, but also the time involved in contract negotiation and other costs of conducting the early outsourcing life-cycle stages.

3. Know your market

Knowing your market is akin to knowing your environment – the playground, so to speak. As an example, consider a sports analogy. Suppose you are Manchester United, Liverpool, Arsenal or any of the premier English football clubs and are competing for players. What is your market? Is it restricted to the English Premier Division clubs or are you competing against clubs in Europe such as AC Milan in Italy or Ajax in Amsterdam or Barcelona in Spain? What about the second-tier clubs, or the clubs in South America? All of these are markets for players. Each market has advantages and disadvantages in terms of player acquisitions. For instance, if you get a player from South America, the chances are high that you could acquire a decent player at lower cost with fewer legal hassles, as a player would be motivated to play at a bigger stage in Europe. However, you may have to pay a price in terms of getting the player acquainted to the European setting in terms of language, relocation costs, etc. These costs would possibly be lower if you try to recruit a player from a peer-division English club, but the cost savings here would be overshadowed by the legal and acquisition costs; moreover, your room for negotiating on player salaries would be lower. The point here is quite simple – depending on the market and industry in which the vendor operates, there are distinct advantages and disadvantages that need to be accounted for during negotiation. Not recognizing the intricacies of the market will lead to negotiations that are faulty and, at best, incomplete. Moreover, having information about the market gives an organization a sense of what else is out there in terms of options. This is another reason why it is vital to study the various vendor proposals during the vendor-assessment phase and to appreciate their diversity.

4. Prioritize your requirements

While we all want what we need, some needs are more important to us than others. It is important that organizations prioritize their needs up front. This helps them weed out vendors that are going to help meet their core needs and those that are going to help meet needs that are peripheral. Think about buying a suit. If it does not fit you, does it really matter that it meets your color requirements? If it does fit, however, you may be ready to compromise on the color. Not prioritizing requirements leads to a situation in negotiations where one does not know what to focus on.

Four-tier list for requirements

First – Critical
Second – Important
Third – Required
Fourth – Desired but not required

We recommend making a four-tier list for requirements: critical, important, required and desired but not required. Doing so gives you a framework to go about the negotiations. At *no* cost do you negotiate on items that are critical – these must be a part of the contract for you to have an outsourcing deal.

Items that are important are the second tier of requirements and you must strive very hard not to negotiate on these. In most cases, you may be open to different methods for delivery of such requirements, but not their elimination from the contract. For example, if you would like to receive weekly reports e-mailed to the senior managers over-seeing the outsourcing efforts, maybe you will be able to settle for having them posted on an intranet portal. However, you should not agree to have them dropped from the deal.

Items that are required make up the third tier. You will have to nego-tiate to get them included in the deal. Required items, while good to have, are not important or critical, so if there is a reasonable argument as to why they must be modified or altered from their original concep-tions, it will not be a bad idea to compromise.

Desired items are those that are nice to have, like the bells and whistles, but are not really needed. These items may come in at the end of negotiations, near the finalizing stages, to throw in as add-ons.

Depending on your relationship with the vendors you are negoti-ating with, we may even suggest sharing this list up front with them. If you have had business dealings with a vendor, this would be a very good move, because it makes the negotiations more productive and straightforward. Negotiations can mostly center around items that are important and required, rather than critical or desired items.

5. Know your time frame

Negotiations are time-sensitive. If you have a sense of urgency, you may need to negotiate on the top three most important things and compromise on some others. However, if you do have the time, you could probably spend it to get more of the things that are important to you. We do not recommend rushing the negotiations process, but sometimes one just has to. The other thing you need to pay attention to is that a deal offered by the vendor today may not be available tomorrow. Negotiations can continue forever if one wants them to, but at what cost? Is the extra $10,000 of saving on the contract price really

worth another half-day meeting? Probably not, as the cost of the negotiation team's salaries will probably be greater than the cost savings.
Another significant issue about not knowing when to end is the danger
of getting inundated with information and crippled by over-analysis. A
few choices and sufficient information is always an asset during negotiations, while getting inundated with facts and figures will result in
information overload. Hence, persistent negotiations over petty
matters are not recommended.

Negotiations are good and wise, but there must be an end in sight.
An important point worth noting is that an offer that is on the table
today may not be there tomorrow. Put another way, every time you
turn down an offer, it is dead, at least in a legal sense. Hence, it is
important not to overdo negotiations. As a case in point, a manufacturing organization was contemplating outsourcing its information
system maintenance work. After two months of negotiations with the
vendor, they were close to getting an agreement in place. To their
dismay, one morning the senior member of the negotiation team
received a call from the vendor stating that they were not going to be
pursuing the outsourcing effort – so close! The previous evening, the
vendor had learnt that three of its current significant clients were re-
signing their agreements and extending their contracts, so what
seemed like good business with the manufacturing company now no
longer looked that good. And, since the manufacturing firm declined
on the last offer made during the previous negotiation discussions,
they had no legal recourse to pursue with the vendor. The lesson: be
wary of extending the negotiation period indefinitely. Have an end
in sight.

6. Start from your position then move towards the vendor's

Most car dealers in the United States display a MSRP (manufacturer
suggested retail price). No one ever pays that price. However, there
are two strategies to negotiating the price: either start with your price
and then move in the direction of the MSRP; or start with the MSRP
and then move down towards your price. Which one is better? If you
choose the first, you have a better chance of getting the car near the
price that you desire; with the second your vendor has a better
chance of securing a price closer to his ideal mark-up. Why?
Negotiations always involve moving to some middle ground. How

much to the 'middle' depends on where one starts. This is why it is important to make sure that you know yourself and establish your position right from the start. Consider the case of Wal-Mart. Any supplier that wants to do business with it is essentially at the mercy of the retail giant. Wal-Mart's position is clearly evident and all of its suppliers know it. If they want to continue to do business with this colossus of the retail world, they must move closer to what Wal-Mart wants rather than dreaming about Wal-Mart moving closer to their position. It is always better to start with your desired price as the baseline and move up from there, rather than taking the vendor's quote and moving down.

7. Have the right negotiation team

A negotiation team should comprise staff members who have broad rather than deep domain knowledge. By this, we mean that you need not have subject matter experts comprise the negotiation team; instead you must focus on having people who can see the big picture – the overall architecture of the outsourcing relationship. Having people who see the broad overview will allow the organization to have a negotiation team that will fight for what is important at the strategic level, rather than the nitty-gritty operational details. The negotiation team is very similar to the team that conducted the strategic assessment of the organization, the only difference being that rather than having it composed exclusively of senior executives; it could be supervised by a senior-level executive and be composed of members from the different functional areas, including the legal, financial, operations, information systems, procurement and human resource divisions.

A vital part of any negotiation team is the legal counsel. Managing the legal staff is a very important part of good negotiations. The legal staff knows the in and outs of contracting, assigning responsibilities, drafting documents, etc. However, they are less skilled at negotiating. Negotiating through lawyers is most often an unfruitful process as it signals excessive formality and lack of trust between the business partners. Lawyers should be keen observers during the negotiations and should share their opinion with the negotiation team over a private meeting. This way, they can get their voices and opinions to the vendor and warn the negotiation team about issues that call for caution.

8. Appreciate cultural differences – organizational and national

At least one member on the negotiation team, or ideally all the members, should have a background in aspects of organizational culture. No two organizations are the same and hence each organization will have different ways of conducting work. Corporate culture most often governs the way work is done in the organization. Hence, to appreciate properly the contextual issues associated with negotiating with a vendor, it is very important to appreciate the vendor's culture. Some vendors may come in dressed in designer suits; others may like the jeans and t-shirt getup. Does that mean one is more competent than the other? Probably not, though if you had posed the question to executives a decade ago, many would not even have allowed the ones in jeans and t-shirts to make a presentation. The recent dot.com and technology revolutions have changed that.

Moreover, if the vendor is based in another country, one must be cognizant about the foreign culture issues. 'When in Rome, do as the Romans do!' Negotiations are about exchanging ideas and fostering agreements via conversation. In order to engage in a successful negotiation practice, it is very important that each party has mutual respect, and much of this respect comes from an understanding about cultural expectations. Norms, taboos and expected practices are unique to most countries. Lack of awareness about these things, or disrespecting them, will lead to a disastrous business relationship.

9. Document, document, document!

The negotiation process can be long and sometimes confusing. What is said today may not be the same as what was said yesterday and might not be what is said tomorrow. This is especially the case when each party is making promises and negotiating various aspects of the contract deal. It is hence of utmost importance that all conversations are documented. This can be done by having a note taker as part of the negotiation team or by having a recap or closing meeting at the end of each day to get the main points down on paper. Documenting the discussions helps build continuity into the negotiation process and also allows one to go back and check up on things promised in the past. This is especially important when two different members from the vendor's team promise two different items that are in conflict with one another. Here, the crucial question becomes: Whose promise supersedes whose? Moreover, when moving into the contract composition stage, the documents from the negotiations will be a good aid in the preparation of a solid contract. Documenting the daily negotiations should include preparing a summary of what was discussed, key items that were resolved and action items that need to be attended to before the next meeting.

10. Negotiate towards a relationship not a contract

Negotiations should be viewed in the broader context of forging a business relationship, not just getting the most advantageous contract signed. Most organizations make a fundamental error here, trying to put all their energies into getting a contract signed for the lowest price. Well, we have seen the prevalence of the 'you get what you pay for' phenomenon. Most outsourcing projects are not one-time deals. They evolve over time, from simple projects to more complex endeavors. One of the reasons why outsourcing projects may evolve is the continuous building of trust between the vendor and client organizations. This trust starts to take shape during the initial negotiation periods. We urge executives to see beyond the cost issues and get to the heart of the relationship – improved business performance for the client and beneficial new business opportunities for the vendor. Building a stable and good relationship calls for both parties to make compromises, some of which may include paying a price that is higher than originally expected. However, if the payment is well spent and a fruitful business relationship matures, organizations will recoup the costs very quickly. On the other hand, if the negotiations are fierce and unfriendly and the vendor is not happy with its end of the deal, the chances are that it might take the deal just to get the short-term revenue, but with no sense of a long-term relationship. In a few months, the client organization will have to shell out more money to conduct the new needs-analysis and vendor-selection processes.

Another not-so-subtle point is that if you negotiate towards a relationship and not a contract, you have a chance of renegotiating the current contract in the future. Renegotiations are commonplace in most outsourcing endeavors; one reason being that it is difficult to plan for everything at the onset. There will always be things that slip the planning phase and only arise when the contract is in operation, either during the project transition or the governance phase. This is where it is valuable to have an established relationship with the vendor and not a relationship with the contract! If the client has a healthy relationship with the vendor, chances are that both parties can renegotiate a contract that is mutually favorable.

Contract management

Once negotiations end in an agreement the next logical step is to document the agreement – produce the contract. Outsourcing contracts can range in depth, detail, form and duration. However, good contracts are clear, concise, complete and have well-defined statements on how the client and vendor organizations will meet each other's business outcomes and expectations. We will begin with a discussion of the various types of contract.

Types of outsourcing contract

Several types of outsourcing contract are currently used (see Table 6.1). They include time and material, fixed-price, shared risk and reward, cost-plus and utility-based contracts.

Time and material contracts are when the vendor prices its services based on a predetermined negotiated hourly labor rate and charges back the actual costs for additional materials to the client. These types of contract are common in most endeavors. For example, if you take your BMW to the garage for repairs, you are charged at the hourly rate for the mechanics plus any parts required for the repairs. Time and materials contracts are normally good for short-term, well-defined engagements. Here you do not want to negotiate on the pricing, as it is not worthwhile in terms of the scope of the project. Moreover, you will not envision the work to be recurrent and long term. Hence, you are not so concerned about establishing a long-term relationship with the vendor. You could use one vendor today and if the need arises in future you may go to another vendor who might offer a lower hourly rate and other discounts. The primary concern when engaging in a time and materials contract is the ability of the vendor to deliver a quality product or service on schedule.

Table 6.1 Types of outsourcing contract

Type of contract	Description
Time and material	The vendor prices its services based on a predetermined hourly labor rate and charges back the actual costs for additional materials to the client
Fixed-price	The vendor provides the client a fixed-price bid for the proposed project or service based on a client-provided statement of work
Shared risk and reward	Contracts that mutually align the organizations' business objects and spread risk and reward
Cost-plus	Contracts negotiated based on predetermined vendor profits guaranteed over the actual vendor costs
Utility-based	Contracts priced on a pay-as-you-go basis

Fixed-price contracts are when the vendor provides the client a fixed-price bid for the proposed project or service, based on a client-provided SOW. The vendor will charge for additional services that are outside the scope of the SOW. Fixed-price contracts involve up-front negotiations with the vendor to come up with an agreed price. These contracts are preferable to a basic time and materials contract when clients have a well-defined project that is large enough to get discounts. For example, if you knew that your BMW is due for its 60,000 mile service, you would opt to pay a fixed price for the service package, rather than go for a time and materials arrangement where you would have to pay for each individual item. On the fixed-price basis, you will get a discounted rate for the overall package. If, however, your car just needed a simple oil change or new tire, you would prefer to pay the hourly rate and stick to the time and materials contract. The underlying premise for a fixed-price contract is to get discounts associated with purchasing items in bundles or packages. Organizations therefore need to know exactly what they want in order to define the package and seek the appropriate discounts from the vendor. Once the package is defined, and the contract is signed, to add an additional item to the package will be expensive and in some cases eat up the original discount secured by the fixed-price contract.

Shared risk and reward contracts are becoming much more common in the past few years, as clients and vendors have become more experienced in structuring outsourcing contracts and look for contract structures that mutually align the organizations' business objectives and spread risk and rewards between both parties. These contractual agreements have financial penalties and incentives aligned to overall business objectives. The goals of penalties and incentives are to encourage vendors to resolve problems and drive for continuous improvements and innovations that promote the achievement of the outsourcing objectives.

The types of penalty that may be imposed include:

- credits against future payments, to compensate for work that does not adhere to contracted requirements but has already been paid for by a reduction in future payments;
- delayed payments, where payment for current work is delayed until a problem is resolved;
- cash penalties, in the form of reduction in payments to the vendor owing to failure to meet a contractual obligation.

The types of incentive that may be considered are:

- performance-based pricing where, when performance in a given time period exceeds some specified criteria, additional payments are applied; when it falls short, penalties are imposed;
- gain sharing, where the vendor receives a portion of any additional savings it can generate for the outsourcing project through its effort;
- achievement bonuses that are usually one-time payments provided for reaching certain outsourcing objectives, which may be tied to earlier than expected completion dates, better than expected throughput or higher than committed service levels.

We believe that risks and rewards contracts will continue to grow in structuring outsourcing relationships as both clients and vendors look to spread risk and drive mutually beneficial business objectives. The objective of these contracts is to compensate the vendor for superior performance. Penalties must be used if necessary to get the vendor back on track but not so as to create financial hardship that cripples the vendor organization and threatens the viability of the outsourcing relationship.

Cost-plus contracts are negotiated based on predetermined vendor profits guaranteed over the actual vendor costs. These contracts are usually best suited for feasibility studies or research projects where a great degree of latitude is given to the vendor to investigate and research various solution alternatives. Cost-plus contracts need to be managed very closely, because all the cost risks of the project are borne by the client organization as the vendor has no incentive to keep costs down and is guaranteed a profit over its actual project costs.

Utility-based contracts are priced on a pay-as-you-go basis, rated on actual usage of the service by the clients. These contracts are the most dynamic and flexible and are growing in number because they offer speed, cost savings and flexibility. In addition, this is a really attractive alternative for small and medium-sized companies that do not want to invest in equipment, people and processes – again, the advantage of variable costs over fixed costs. There have also been improvements in security, pricing and customization options as the business model has matured. As an analogy, consider the following. If you pay rent for a villa, you have a fixed-price contract. Regardless of how many days you actually live in it, or even use it at all, you pay a monthly fee. Now, consider renting a hotel room. A hotel room is a utility-based contract. Here, you pay a premium for the use of the room – the cost of staying in a hotel for one night is always greater than the comparable cost of renting accommodation. However, if as part of a particular trip you were planning short visits to several different locations, renting a villa in every place would just not be feasible, as the costs would be enormous. Hence, you engage in utility-based contracts for short-term assignments. You pay as needed, with little up-front investment or maintenance costs. Today, utility-based computing is popular. Under this mechanism, organizations can rent software applications, hardware, network space and other utilities for a price, with minimal hassle, to meet sudden surges in computing demands.

Outsourcing contracts have developed to best meet the growing demands of offshore project requirements. Time and material contracts are best suited when requirements are not well defined and details on scope, level of effort and performance are still in a state of flux. Fixed-price contracts are used when requirements and statements of works are defined and mutually agreed upon by both client and vendor. Here, clients need to understand that changes in requirements may impact costs, schedule or performance. Shared risk and reward contracts are used to mitigate and share the risks of outsourcing projects between the client and vendor and elicit behavior that advance the achievements of outsourcing project goals and objectives. Cost-plus contracts, although not as common as in the past, may be good alternatives for initial feasibility studies or loosely-defined research projects. Utility-based contracts are becoming more common as companies look to minimize their infrastructure, people and process costs as well as look for outsourcing structures that improve time to market and organizational flexibility. Outsourcing contracts will continue to evolve as the mechanism to codify the outsourcing relationship.

Components of the outsourcing contract

The outsourcing contract must clearly describe:

- the scope and nature of the engagement;
- roles and responsibilities of the client organization;
- roles and responsibilities of the vendor organization;
- metrics for evaluating the performance of the relationship;
- recourses in case things do not go as expected.

Most outsourcing contracts are made up of five parts:

- a master contract;
- operating principles;
- metrics definition;
- SOWs;
- SLAs.

The master contract, also called the principal or framework document, defines the overall legal arrangement of the relationship between the vendor and client organizations. The operating principles establish the accepted norms of behavior and also define boundaries about what is acceptable. In doing so, they set the boundary on what is not permitted in the outsourcing relationship. The metrics definitions state agreed measures for evaluating performance on the part of vendor and client organizations. As a simple example, it may clearly state that the two organizations will use the decimal system for calculations or that a year for business purposes is defined as 280 days, etc. The SOWs and SLAs are documents that codify the specifics, the

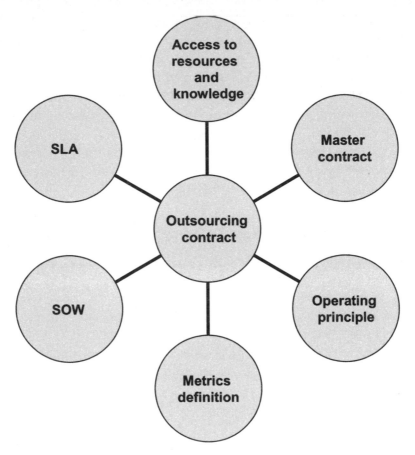

Figure 6.1 Components of the outsourcing contract

nitty-gritty, so to speak. They talk in specific terms about the project, its tasks, resource usages and expected ranges of expected performance for the tasks. These documents are more fluid and dynamic compared to the preceding three and can change multiple times during the business relationship; moreover, they will change depending on the project being outsourced. We will now explore each of the components in further detail.

The master contract

The master contract is a legal document that codifies the rules by which the client and the vendor will operate throughout the duration of the outsourcing engagement. There is usually one master contract that governs the entire relationship. It contains the financial terms of the agreement and standard legal protection and covers topics such as issue resolution, work requirement changes, intellectual property ownership, and dispute resolution and exit clauses from a legal perspective.

The master contract does not describe the specific details of the assignment to be performed; these are described in project-related metrics, SOWs and SLAs. Those related documents can be changed, new assignments can be added and existing assignments can be dropped by modifying the affected documents rather than by changing the master contract. The master contract will specify the rules for when, how and for what compensation such changes can be made.

Operating principles

The operating principles define how the vendor and the client are going to work together on a daily basis throughout the life of the contract. These principles cover the logistics of the engagement, paying special attention to handoffs between the vendor and the client. Subjects covered in this document include reporting protocols, governance procedures and processes for activities such as submitting reports, work requests and problem escalation.

Important items to include in the operating principles include:

- the nature of the communications plan – how often you and the vendors will meet to discuss the outsourcing relationship, whether these meetings will be face-to-face or virtual and how information will be relayed between the two organizations in terms of ad-hoc or emergency instances;
- a change-management process – how training will be handled and who will be responsible for managing the change process in the organization;
- a problem-escalation process – how problems and issues will get resolved, who will be the contact person for the two organizations, a proposed forum for resolving disputes, how awards may be enforced, arbitration methods and how problems will escalate to the managerial levels should they not get resolved;
- a performance-appraisal process – how performance will be evaluated and how evaluations will be incorporated into improvement of the outsourcing relationship;

- a business continuity provision, which is a developed, detailed plan that requires transfer of data in the case of disaster, a provision to transfer key staff for continuity, business continuity drill procedures;
- a security plan to ensure protection of intellectual property during the contract.

Metrics definition

Metrics help organizations evaluate how the operating principles are being conducted by providing measures to show the compliance and level of compliance to each item. It is important to note that it is not just compliance to the operating principles that organizations must be concerned with. More important is the issue of *consistency* in the level of compliance. Is the vendor consistently upholding the operating principles? A vendor that only sporadically upholds operating principles may be no better than one that avoids them altogether.

Depending on its use and objectives, a given metric may be collected by the vendor, the client or an impartial third party. Specifying the metric in detail ensures that it will be collected and interpreted consistently throughout the project. A metric's definition includes its name, description, objectives, measurement method, rules for initialization and responsibility and roles for collection and interpretation. When defining metrics, choose metrics in the right context to the job at hand. Choose metrics that are realistic for both sides, and are easy to collect, analyze and manage. Two major categories to include in metrics are the level of effort that the vendor provides within the project scope and the number of units of deliverables generated within a given time frame. Factors you need to consider are the number of defects in major deliverables, the vendor's service availability and your level of satisfaction as well as time to market, cost per unit of work produced and allocation of resources.

SOWs

As discussed in Chapter 4, an SOW defines the scope of the project by specifying the assets and/or functions supported, the types of work to be performed, the inputs required, the deliverables to be created and the roles of each party in the effort. SOWs vary widely in format, content and usage from project to project. An outsourcing agreement may have one large SOW encompassing the entire effort or a series of SOWs describing discrete portions of the effort. Unless the engagement is limited in scope and complexity, a single 'do everything'

SOW quickly becomes cumbersome to create and administer. Using multiple SOWs provides more flexibility by allowing each project portion to have its own parameters and to be adjusted independently of the other. Remember that an SOW should have enough detail to ensure that the vendor and the client have a clear understanding of their responsibilities and the deliverables that will be produced.

SLAs

The SLA defines the parameters by which work will be performed and judged. SLAs are matched to project-specific SOWs. Each major task and work product in an SOW has a related performance criterion in an SLA. The SLA specifies criteria such as the volume of work that should be completed within a given time frame, acceptable response time for requests, quality requirements and measures of efficiency.

The performance criteria for each work product are described using metrics. These metrics must be carefully selected to provide an accurate measure of performance from the view of the final recipient of the work product or service being delivered. Generally, separate metrics are used for each characteristic being measured. Penalty and reward structures are used to motivate all parties to live up to their SLA commitments. Although the mechanics of these structures are defined within the contract, rewards and penalties for specific deliverables are identified within the SLA. This approach ensures that penalties and rewards are updated whenever the SLA is adjusted. The number of SLAs and their level of detail should match the number and level of detail of SOWs. As described above for the SOW, there is a tradeoff between flexibility and ongoing measurement and reporting overhead.

The SLA is one of the key pieces of the outsourcing contract. The performance metrics used in the SLA must reflect your organization's expected performance over the life of the engagement. The metrics used must be objective and unambiguous to both your organization and the vendor's. These include operating principles to define and document daily procedures throughout the life of the contract.

Essentials of composing an adequate contract

An outsourcing contract is the result of detailed due diligence and objective assessment by the client organization. It assesses the current-state strengths, weaknesses and core competencies of its business. It also assesses the organization's future requirements in which a decision has been made, based on objective criteria and business needs, to source products and/or services to a third-party vendor. The outsourcing contract is a combination of specific documents (master contract, operating principles, metrics, SOWs and SLAs) that describes to both the client and vendor the nature and scope of the relationship, specific project requirements and management framework (especially change management) throughout the life of the contract. Hidden costs can usually be traced to not conducting the proper due diligence and organization assessment prior to moving forward in the identification, evaluation and selection of the vendor. This usually manifests itself in an incomplete contract and product requirements, which will create conflict between the client and vendor organizations resulting in a misalignment of expectations, excessive change management and excessive organizational disputes. Many organizations do not invest the time and resources, nor have the specific skills, to conduct a detailed due diligence and objective organization assessment. One of the key cornerstones of any successful outsourcing relationship is to understand where you are today and where you need to be in the future.

Contracts are legal documents that must be detailed yet manageable, comprehensive yet cohesive and specific yet flexible. Writing a contract is an art and that is why some contracting experts are some of the highest paid knowledge professionals today. Some guidelines to bear in mind when composing the contract are discussed below.

Essentials of composing an adequate contract

Ensure comprehensiveness
Assign responsibilities clearly
Include the exit strategy
Avoid vendor-standard contracts

Ensure comprehensiveness

Typically, it is better to include more information rather than less. Be comprehensive in the contract and write the contract so as to include all 'material matters', to borrow a term from the accounting and auditing literature. What is a material matter? When writing or compiling financial statements, they must be free from 'material misstatement', ie significant transactions that can alter the financial picture of the organization should not be left out. Similar rules apply to writing an outsourcing contract. All material matters need to be clearly stated and included in the outsourcing contract. Once again, if it is not on paper it may not be part of the business relationship.

While you do want to be comprehensive, you must know when you have gone too far. Horror or success stories are usually based on the vendor's and client's outsourcing maturity level in contracting. The contract is a document, after all, and it is what transpires around the document that is of value and will be the crux of the business relationship. It is important for both parties to understand that the contract is a framework that governs the operations of the relationship. Problems arise when a client tries to specify every element of the relationship and each specific project in a prescriptive manner and the vendor looks for ways to push risk back to the client. This can lead to extended contract negotiating time frames and bad blood between the parties before the contract is even signed. There must be trust and a shared risk between the client and the vendor. This requires a long-term partnership mentality. The most success we have had is with organizations that understand this and the mutual business benefits to both organizations. This mindset has to be established at the executive level and driven down throughout both the client and vendor organizations prior to sitting down and negotiating a contract. It has been our experience that if the mutual business benefits are clearly understood from the start, the contract negotiations proceed smoothly.

Assign responsibilities clearly

The contract must be clear on who does what. There should be no ambiguity in responsibility assignment. Responsibility assignments include matters of the outsourcing project such as task completions, fixing errors or defects and resource procurement and should also cover matters outside the project such as financial obligations and legal recourses. Failure to assign clear responsibilities will result in finger pointing and lawsuits. Most courts will not take kindly to having to clear up sloppy contracting and may, in many cases, just throw the case out, as they do not know whom to believe and the contract lacks credibility as a legal document. The contract, in terms of assignment of responsibilities, must be as clear to a layperson of reasonable intelligence as it is to an experienced lawyer. An acid test is to give the contract to someone other than a legal person and ask him or her to go through it and outline who does what, based on his or her reading of the document. If the person comes up with fewer items than what you intended or items different from what you intended, the contract is not complete and needs to be redrafted.

Include an exit strategy

Document an exit strategy up front. Include answers to questions like:

- Should things go bad, how will the business relationship end?
- Who will be paid what?
- How will the assets be returned?
- How will work-in-progress be handled?

These issues are significant and if not planned for up front will lead to one of two disastrous outcomes. First, if the relationship goes sour, as client you are locked in and at the mercy of the vendor due to lack of an exit strategy. Second, the relationship goes sour; you can exit the relationship, but you have no backup plan in place to ensure continuity of work. Both these cases are manageable and the losses one may incur can be mitigated by up-front planning.

Organizations are urged to come up with an exit strategy before signing the contract. The key questions for organizations are:

- Assuming that the contract is signed and the relationship fails, how do we pull out and ensure minimum disruption to our business?
- What if the relationship fails in three months? Six months? Nine months? Another time period?

Having multiple exit strategies depending on various time frames will help managers think through issues such as the level of the intensity of the outsourcing relationship, the severity of resource commitment, the difficulty in pulling out in the later as compared to early stages and other important issues.

Avoid vendor-standard contracts

It is important not to fall prey to vendor-standardized contracts. Each vendor has a filing cabinet full of these and will be the first to suggest that you sign one. Common reasons given for signing a vendor's standard contract are that it will take too long or involve too much effort to write a unique one, the vendor's contract is applicable to the current business, many other clients have not had any problems with it, etc. An organization should always have its own legal people in charge of drafting the contract, to help ensure that it has ultimate control over what goes in and what stays out of the contract. Relinquishing control over who writes the contract is a serious error.

Conclusion and checklist

The nature of outsourcing contracts is bound to change as organizations get more comfortable with the outsourcing of knowledge work and more complex forms of projects. Owing to the complexity of outsourcing relationships, there has been a growing realization that outsourcing contracts cannot be prescriptive and detailed down to every potential 'what if' of the relationship. Outsourcing contracts are evolving into flexible frameworks of how to describe and manage the overall relationship that includes both mutual benefits and shared risks between the client and vendor organizations. These are living, breathing documents that will evolve and need to be actively managed in the dynamic global world we live in.

The outsourcing contract that describes the business, legal and technical aspects of the client–vendor relationship must be flexible and must be dynamically managed. A good outsourcing contract is the result of a detailed due diligence, organization assessment and vendor identification, evaluation and selection by the client organization prior to formalizing a contract. It reflects mutual benefits and shared risks for both the client and vendor organization and is understood by all parties involved. It defines for both the client and vendor organizations the current, future and termination elements of the outsourcing relationship. It will be the document that both organizations will refer to for help in managing the outsourcing relationship throughout the life of the contract.

Organizations must be steadfast and diligent in investing the time, resources and experience in the early outsourcing life-cycle phases (strategic assessment, needs analysis and vendor assessment) to ensure that they understand the ramification of moving forward with their outsourcing initiative (business, legal, technical, human resources). Once the contract is signed, it is very difficult to right any wrongs that are a result of missed or misinterpreted expectations or requirements.

The outsourcing contract contains and describes key elements and requirements that are required to implement a thorough ongoing program for project initiation, transition and governance. In the governance life-cycle phase, the contract describes key performance measures, goals and targets that will be reviewed and reported. In addition, the contract will describe standard procedures to conduct periodic audits on processes, procedures, methodologies and service level data that will be monitored in the project transition and governance phases of the outsourcing life cycle. The following questions provide a checklist for contract management:

- Is there a negotiation team in place that understands the needs of the outsourcing project, the vendor and the marketplace?
- Have you prioritized your needs?
- Is there a time frame for negotiations?
- Is there an established documentation process to capture items discussed during negotiations?
- Do you understand the broader business relationship value so that you can negotiate towards it?
- Do you understand the various types of contract? And can you choose the right one for your purpose?
- Does your contract cover the major sections of master contract, operating principles, metrics, SOWs and SLAs?

7 Project initiation and project transition

After signing the contract an organization is not ready to put the outsourcing relationship in motion. It is best to study the outsourcing relationship in three stages. First, the client has to initiate or start the project, which can be considered the immediate period following the signing of the contract. Next, begins the transition of the project, where the client organization begins to relinquish control and the vendor begins to take control of the project. The third stage is managing the ongoing relationship to ensure that it meets with the original expectations and to improve the relationship as needed. The first two stages will be covered in this chapter; the third stage is the subject of the next chapter.

Project initiation is where a client organization puts the foot to the pedal and begins outsourcing the work. This stage can be best described as one of chaos and chaotic issues. Even in the best outsourcing deals, things are bound to get a bit rough during this initial phase. But organizations should not despair – a little healthy friction at the start of the relationship is a good thing, as it means that both parties care enough about the business relationship to do their part in making it work. We would actually be surprised if there were *no* overt friction and if no issues surfaced. This might mean that someone is actually not doing the work, or worse, critical issues are being hidden from one party or the other. Both of these are early signs of a disastrous outsourcing relationship. Early friction can be a good thing if managed appropriately, but if left to its own devices and unmanaged, it will sow the seeds of acrimony between the two parties, which in turn will come back to haunt both parties in the future. There is only one area of focus during the initiation stage – getting the outsourcing relationship operational and to that point of stability where the client can actually begin to relinquish control to the vendor.

Relinquishing control to the vendor occurs during the transition stage. Here, you work with the background put in place at the initiation phase and start to move the work outside. This process can be easy or awkward, depending much on the work you have done during the initiation stage. The focus of this stage is to *transition* work, decision rights and knowledge to the vendor organization, so that it can conduct the work effectively and, for the most part, independently from your organization. After all, if the vendor can never work on its own and you still have to pay attention to managing the project, you lose one of the most critical benefits of outsourcing, ie the cost savings associated with sourcing out the tasks. Moreover, you might end up doing work that you are paying the vendor for, thereby incurring two expenses – the cost of the contract and the opportunity cost of conducting the tasks. In the final analysis, the transition stage is the groundwork for the operational acts of conducting the outsourcing project.

Project initiation

This section describes the salient factors to consider during the initial stages of the outsourcing activity. As mentioned above, the initiation stage is one of chaotic dynamics. The first thing that you must do is to acknowledge this and be prepared to be loose and flexible rather than stay rigid. While a good contract and adequate negotiations will help out during project transition and governance, it will have minimal effect on the initiation stage. Think of it this way: when two individuals sign a contract to rent an apartment, this does not mean that the first few days will be frictionless. Each roommate will need to make compromises to get through the first few days and get the living arrangement to some state of normality. Just imagine if the two do not make any special accommodations when each one is moving in – the living arrangement would not get past the first day! However, once the initial period is over, each roommate will expect the other to take care of his

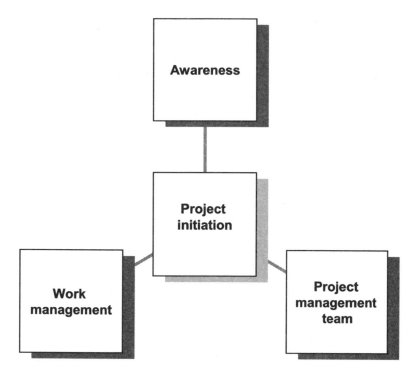

Figure 7.1 Critical issues in project initiation

or her share of responsibilities and uphold his or her individual commitments to the negotiated contract. Similarly, it is important that you do not get too excited about the outsourcing contract during the initial period and instead focus your energies on getting a working relationship in order, even if you have to make costly accommodations at the outset. For this, you need to pay attention to several factors (see Figure 7.1).

Awareness

First, you must make sure that all stakeholders are aware of and familiar with the terms and conditions of the negotiated contract. Once the contract is negotiated and signed, it represents the outsourcing relationship. The contract may not include all of the items that were considered necessary at the time of conducting the needs analysis, because compromises do take place during negotiations. Moreover, the contract may include items not thought of during the earlier stages of the outsourcing life cycle. Consequently, it is important and critical that all stakeholders be educated on the terms and conditions of the contract. This will enable everyone to be on the same page and work as a unit with a common undertaking to make the outsourcing relationship a success. Without having everyone working in unison, there will be lack of common contextual knowledge to foster effective communication among the stakeholders.

Exchanging ideas and communication of information will become difficult, as everyone will have a different idea about what really is transpiring during the initial stage – not having everyone on the same page just adds to the chaos and confusion here. Communication with stakeholders can be achieved by having a series of mandatory seminars offered to senior executives, who must in turn hold meetings with their staff to communicate the necessary information.

Project management team

Second, your organization must establish a team to oversee the project initiation and transition phases of the outsourcing life cycle. This team should comprise domain experts and be managed by a program manager who must oversee the outsourcing project. The analogy we might use is that of building a special operations team for combat. Each member must bring a unique skill that is needed for success and in the case of the armed services this would include skills such as demolitions, sniper shooting and intelligence gathering. While each member has a unique skill, the group *must* work together towards the common goal – winning. Without this common objective, each member's skills will be of no use. Similarly, you need to put in place a strong project management team to lead the outsourcing relationship through the initiation and transition stages. Each member of the team must be an expert in areas such as communication management, culture training, finance, legal matters or IT. This team must be managed as a unit and must have a dedicated 'control center' to oversee the relationship. This control center can be virtual or physical. If virtual, it could be a common website that each member has access to. The website would host current information about the project, issues, resolutions, etc and provide a forum for the members to interact. In a physical control center, the members can have a dedicated room or office space that is used to control the effort – much like a war room.

Work management

Third, you must map out the key tasks that need to be performed. There will a number of tasks that need to be attended to during the initial stages and these must be clearly identified. Once identified, you must look at the dependencies across the tasks to come up with a workable plan. In addition, you must focus on what is important in the immediate period; this requires you to prioritize the list. Not all issues that come up can get due attention in the initial period, so it is important to focus attention on critical matters. It is beneficial to concentrate on a few issues and sort those out, rather than attending to all issues in a haphazard manner and getting nothing resolved.

In dealing with emergent issues or problem areas, you must remember the focus of this phase – to get the relationship going. It is not in the interest of the organization to halt the relationship in the initiation stage to get at the root cause of issues; this will be appropriate during the next stage (transition) and the one that follows (governance). At the initiation stage, it is important to smooth things over and come up with workable fixes to get the relationship on an even keel. You must use 'band-aid solutions' to address problems and get the process moving, as stopping it will result in a loss of momentum for the overall initiative and open up more problems than those you intend to fix. The transition team must thoroughly document the issues it faces during the transition stage and the fixes or solutions applied. In the next stages, these issues and fixes can be revisited and investigated at greater length.

Project transition

Now that you have passed the initial stage of chaos and confusion, it is time to start getting to the crux of the outsourcing engagement by sourcing out control to the vendor. During the transition stage you make this leap and the focus here is to 'iron out the creases'. The critical issues that you must contend with and pay attention to are outlined in Figure 7.2 and discussed below.

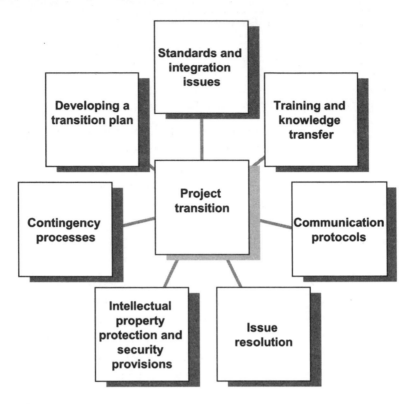

Figure 7.2 Critical issues in project transition

Standards and integration issues

Outsourcing normally involves some aspect of standards and integration work. Two disparate systems need to be combined into one, or one part of the system provided by a vendor needs to be combined with the client's overall system architecture, or there will be another combination or permutation of such integration work. The important issue here is how these aspects are to be managed. We would hope that the standards and parameters of integration work have been covered in the negotiation and contract stages. However, there might be new issues that emerge during the actual implementation. Here, there is only one guideline to follow – enter into an open discussion with the vendor on the pros and cons of the integration and standards challenges, arrive at a solution, then redraft the contract to include this new clause, and continue with the work. Do *not* blindly accept standards such as the use of a particular architecture or operating system and do *not* enforce standards blindly either. Listen to your business partner and ensure that it is listening to you as well, and, as emphasized in the previous chapter, *get things in writing*.

Training and knowledge transfer

It is important to train personnel during the transition stage. Here, you are looking to see what knowledge needs to be transferred to the vendor's staff to enable them better to manage the project. You must be careful in how knowledge is transferred by ensuring that you strike the right balance between transferring too little knowledge and too much.

Transferring too little knowledge will jeopardize how the outsourcing vendor will manage the project. This is because the vendor will not know all the contextual details surrounding the project and will make faulty assumptions about your business operations. Too little knowledge is also dangerous because it impedes communication between you and the vendor due to a lack of common frames of reference. For example, if you and the vendor use jargon or technical terms to communicate with each other without a proper appreciation of the significance of those terms in each other's context, the transfer of knowledge will be faulty. Transferring too much knowledge is equally dangerous because it opens up the possibility that knowledge losses may occur, jeopardizing your competitive edge. The larger the number of people let in on a secret, the greater is the chance that it will no longer be a secret. The organization should be clear on the kind of knowledge that needs to be shared and knowledge that should remain private. We will discuss the issues of security measures in a forthcoming section that complements the discussion about knowledge transfer and knowledge protection here.

As for training, both you and the vendor must make commitments towards effective knowledge transfer. The ideal strategy would be to create a team of experts comprising members from your organization and the vendor's. This joint team or task force can be responsible for training both organizations. While it helps when the person training you is someone from your organization whom you are familiar with, it is even better when you see a training team that is truly integrated so as to signify a united business relationship. Moreover, having members from the other organization will help in answering questions for which you may not have an answer and also in putting a face to the other organization. These small matters make a big difference in how the outsourcing relationship is perceived.

The other point about training is to have informal mechanisms in place to foster the exchange of information and knowledge. This is very easy to do with computer support. Organizations can build an extranet, an internet resource that is shared by the vendor and the client. They can use this platform to set up discussion groups, document repositories, FAQs and other mechanisms that promote informal interactions among employees in both organizations. This can be an excellent way for people to connect with one another and also find ways to getting at knowledge that complements the formal training methods. Remember that knowledge flows are enhanced when the source and recipient share mutual trust and respect and know one another, rather than when two strangers are interacting.

Communication protocols

Among the many issues to iron out during the transition stage, communication protocols are perhaps the most crucial. Consider the following as a case in point. One of us researched an outsourcing project to help a medium-sized IT consulting organization to systematize their post-mortem analysis efforts. This project was so fraught with communication failures that it was labeled 'Project Misunderstanding' (Desouza, Dingsøyr and Awazu, 2005). The project involved 20 software engineers, 5 systems analysts, 2 quality assurance personnel and a project manager, lasted for eight months and involved interaction between staff members at the US corporate office and the offshore staff in India.

Since the design and development was handled offshore, the US-based workgroup had the responsibility for requirements gathering, final testing and delivery. Over 20 critical misunderstandings occurred between the phases of requirements gathering and design and most of these could be attributed to the poor standards of documentation, usage of localized jargon and making assumptions on what knowledge was possessed by the team in India. The initial meeting between the staff based in the United States and India never occurred. The reason was simple – no one specified the reference time. An excerpt of the e-mail from the US project manager said, 'let us schedule a meeting for 4 – OK?', the response from the team leader in India went, 'sure ... see you then'. Never was it clearly specified whether this was 4 AM or PM and in what time zone. During the postmortem, the root-cause analysis for this problem was established to be no clear agreement on communication conventions. One of the recommendations from the project postmortem was to specify clearly communication conventions such as the use of English or metric system, time conventions and reference time zone.

Misunderstanding also occurred when sensitive issues were incorrectly interpreted. The two teams had problems signifying items such as urgency, need for punctuality, explanation facilities and responses to e-mails. For example, if the Indian developer wanted clarification on an item, in an e-mail he or she would almost never use the word 'urgent' but would write 'I would appreciate it if you could answer this at your earliest convenience'. To the US employees, 'earliest convenience' meant that the matter was not urgent and a delayed response would be acceptable.

Among the many things to sort out during the transition stage, communication protocols are the most salient. Failure to communicate effectively is one of the most commonly cited reasons for outsourcing failures. It is important to agree upon communication conventions by specifying important issues. For example, what is meant by 'urgent'? And if a matter is urgent does one call or send an e-mail; how long should the average response time be; what happens if the primary contact is not available; and who is the secondary contact? What happens when an issue arises for which there is no set person in charge? Is the issue made available to all members of the team or is it only conveyed to the project manager who then decides the right channel? These are very important issues that need to be worked out at the start.

Another matter is the issue of training. The chances are high that most outsourcing projects involve members from different countries. Each country has its own culture and other norms. For instance, most managers in the United States do not quite get the fact that 'The American Way' is not THE way. Certainly, it is *one* of the ways, but not the primary or most prevalent or best way. Similarly, expectations of how individuals communicate must be appreciated in the context of their culture. This is important if organizations are going to have smooth interactions.

Issue resolution

In the initiation stage the focus was on providing temporary 'band-aid solutions' to problems so as to get the project flowing. Now, you must get to the root cause of issues. It is absolutely critical that you do not get into a habit of only applying temporary fixes to problems and now invest time to get to the crux of the problems – treat the disease instead of the symptom, as it were. Success in identifying the problem and its cause will depend on the presence of adequate communication channels and effective knowledge sharing. Problems that are not attended to and fixed during the transition stage will result in building a poor foundation for the future relationship.

It is important to remember that it is easier to fix things at the start of the transition phase. For example, if you do not like the way the vendor communicates its status reports, you can discuss the issue straight away and work out a better solution. However, once the vendor's behavior becomes accepted practice or the norm, changing it will be difficult. After all, the vendor has invested time formalizing this process and will be less open to changing it, as there is greater cost involved in making the change. Many times, this cost will be charged back to the client, either directly as extra fees for the contract, or indirectly, through the vendor's irritations and frustrations which will adversely affect the quality of the outsourcing work.

Intellectual property protection and security provisions

During transition, the organization opens itself to the vendor and this revelation is essential to get the transition process going. However, in doing so, there is the possibility that the client organization may lose valuable intellectual property and other assets if adequate security measures are not in place. Yes, this does happen, and it is a very real issue that you must be wary about. Too often security concerns in an outsourcing relationship are some of the last to be attended to, just because there are other more glamorous issues claiming your attention.

The experienced and mature organization will take prudent steps to ensure that a vendor has access to required material and *only* to required material – on a 'need-to-know' basis, to borrow a term from the defense and government intelligence arenas. Vendors should only be given access to knowledge and critical assets that they need to operate and nothing else. To cite a common occurrence, many client organizations involved in the outsourcing IT work provide involved personnel at the vendor's site with passwords to their system so that programming work can be done. This is a good practice and ensures that only authorized people associated with the vendor are going to be accessing the system. However, there is an important issue that many organizations forget to pay enough attention to – the log in statistic sheet. In one case that we are aware of, an account name, let's say 'John Smith', at the outsourcing vendor's organization logged in from three different office locations in the vendor's country. This is akin to having a person physically log in from London, then within three minutes log in from Liverpool and about ten minutes later log in from Manchester! With a little investigative work, it was uncovered that the vendor had underpriced the contract and not disclosed complete resource allocation numbers; hence the vendor had staff working on the project who were not accounted for in the project plans. According to the contract, the vendor organization was given only 20 passwords to the system for the 20 developers allocated to the project and so had to share passwords between employees so as not to tip-off the client to the actual number of people working on the project. This is a major intellectual property issue.

The client organization cannot afford to take a naive approach to protecting its assets. Your motto must be 'Respect, but suspect'. You must respect the vendor, but at the same time have a watchful eye on its activities. A simple analogy comes to mind. Allied nations routinely spy on their peers along with using espionage tactics on hostile nations, merely because they want to ensure their security by verifying that all is well.

Several essential activities are needed to establish and implement an adequate security plan. First, an organization must tag its assets; these include both physical assets (such as computer equipment) and intangible assets (such as computer files and intellectual property documents). Next, a decision must be made as to which assets need to be accessed by the vendor. Third, efforts must be made to isolate these assets from the rest in order to minimize any interactions or negative effects. For example, if the organization needs to provide the vendor with access to certain software and files, it will be prudent to load these on a separate computer server that is detached from the rest of the organization's information resources. In the worst case, if anything were to go wrong the effects would be confined to the one server, rather than having cascading effects on the overall information systems architecture. Finally, the organization must assign responsibilities, authority and accountability. The client must have people who are responsible for ensuring that security protocols are monitored on a regular basis. If violations do occur, they have the requisite authority to act and if they fail to they will be held accountable.

Contingency processes

It is also important to have a contingency plan in place. This contingency plan should focus on a critical issue – ensuring that there are backups in place should the transition go haywire. For example, a client organization should plan for how it is to proceed if the two systems it is trying to integrate do not get integrated; if the work is delayed by two weeks; if the vendor has problems getting started; and if the vendor's systems crash due to the overload of new transactions. A number of issues can go wrong during the transition phase and these need to be thought of and accounted for in advance, so as to minimize the occurrences of surprises. Organizations need to act based on the probability that a given surprise *will* materialize and use this probability to put contingencies in place to address the issue, should the risk materialize. Obviously, organizations cannot plan for everything. As most people involved in crafting a war plan will tell you, 'No battle plan survives first contact with the enemy', but this does not mean that nations do not plan and just go blindly to war. They plan to account for high-risk items and put in place a framework to guide their behavior should surprise contingencies occur.

Developing a transition plan

All of the matters discussed above need to be documented in a clear and concise manner in a transition plan. This plan should be a stand-alone document that explains how the organization will go about the business of transitioning the project. The transition plan should comprehensively address standards and integration issues, training and knowledge transfer, communication protocols, intellectual property protection and security provisions and the contingency plan. It should place them in a process- and procedure-oriented framework, with enough details on specifics. For instance, in terms of the security measures the transition plan must clearly specify how critical assets will be tagged and monitored; who will be doing the monitoring; what will happen if theft is discovered; and how this matter will be brought to the vendor's attention. In the absence of clearly specified guidelines, people will be left to their own devices about handling situations. In a security consulting project one of us was involved with, an entire security team was fired due to a rather minor issue. The security team that worked for the outsourcing client and was overseeing the transition process noticed a large collection of boxes being moved out of the client's office premises. At first they questioned a few of the staff members who were moving the boxes and were informed that this was agreed upon in the outsourcing contract. Not happy with the answers they got, they decided to halt the movement of the material and wait for executive approval – the right thing to do. However, they could not identify the right executive to call on the matter as no one shared a copy of the transition plan with the security team! To make a long story short, here's the bottom line – the vendor charged the client for the time its work was halted, then had to take an extra two days to catch up on work schedules, the client's work was delayed and key customers of the client were not too happy. As a show of action, the client decided to fire the security team – a stupid move! All due to the lack of care to detail in the transition plan.

This example also brings out another point – a transition plan is not something that has value if it is on paper alone. Its value comes from communicating its existence to the concerned parties, who then actually follow it. The transition plan should therefore be kept action-oriented and brief, yet comprehensive, and made available to all critical units involved in the transition. The transition plan can be thought of as the architect's plan. When constructing the building, each contractor or worker needs to be made aware of the entire architecture and in particular the details of his or her individual assignment. The painter needs to know what color and texture to use, the plumber must know the sewage plan, and so on. All in all, everyone needs to be on the same page, to construct and architect the right relationship.

Key considerations

Questions asked by managers when discussing the stages of project initiation and transition commonly concern timings: How long does the project transition stage last? Will we know when we have transitioned the project or, more important, when it is the right time to transition the project? These are all important issues, but there are no cookbook recipe answers. Each outsourcing project is unique and answers to the above questions will depend on the nature of the project. For example, if your organization has a simple outsourcing project involving the hiring of a vendor to conduct routine maintenance of your information systems, the chances are high that you will be able to transition the project to the vendor after two months. However, if you are outsourcing your entire human resource management function, it may be well past six months before you can successfully relinquish control. The time period will be needed to train the vendor organization, share knowledge with them about your current business practices, conduct adequate change management and retraining of staff and resolve many other necessary details. It is important to realize that while it is a good idea to set aside a time period for project initiation and transition, you must not become restricted by an artificial date or time line. Realize that sometimes you will be able to transition a project quicker than you expect, either because you have had a prior working relationship with the vendor or the vendor's maturity with outsourcing is significant. With other projects, the results may be less than desirable owing to steep learning curves and initial difficulties with getting in sync. It is important to give things time to iron themselves out rather than rushing through them and then dealing with more serious issues later in the relationship, such as in the relationship management stage, which we discuss in the next chapter.

There is another key consideration. While organizations are familiar with most of the other stages of the outsourcing process, as these are common to any sourcing effort from manufacturing to purchasing of office supplies, the project initiation and transition stages and their significance have more critical importance in outsourcing efforts. This is because the clients are actually transitioning knowledge to their vendors and making it a collaborative part of their business.

Owing to the significance of the project initiation and transition stages, it is always a good idea for a client organization to answer the critical question: Have we got the internal expertise to complete the project initiation and transition stages successfully? This question calls for a thorough analysis of the organization's competencies in handling complex projects and being successful in their execution. If an organization has never handled a project of the current magnitude, nor handled issues of transfer of ownership in the past, it is absolutely essential to get external help from skilled and objective professionals. It is not a bad idea to admit that one does not have the required expertise to conduct these stages effectively and bring in experts from the outside. The experts can take the negotiated contract, the outcomes of needs analysis and vendor assessments, along with the strategic assessments, and lead the transition effort. One of the benefits of bringing in an external party at this stage is that they give a fresh set of perspectives, which can help in identifying hidden or critical issues that would otherwise not be discovered, as both the client and vendor organizations are too involved in the nitty-gritty of the outsourcing relationship. One must balance this benefit against the understandable cost of getting the vendor acquainted with the outsourcing relationship so far and – in the case of a vendor that has never worked with the organization before – providing adequate business knowledge so that the vendor can effectively understand the broader context of the outsourcing relationship.

Conclusion and checklist

The process of moving from in-house management of a project to an outsourced provider can be an intimidating challenge. It is a delicate balancing act that involves the entire organization. As outlined in this chapter, there are number of operational and people issues that you must attend to in order to conduct the process effectively. And no sooner is this transition accomplished than you have to manage the ongoing relationship. Prudent planning and execution will not always ensure success, but the failure to do so will almost certainly guarantee disaster. Use the following questions as a checklist for the stages of this process:

- Are all key stakeholders aware of the terms of the negotiated contract?
- Is there a project team in place to oversee the initiation and transition phases?
- Is there a work or task management system in place to oversee the major undertaking during the initiation and transition stages?
- Is there a process in place to handle issues of standardization and integration?

- Are there processes in place to ensure adequate knowledge transfer and training of personnel?
- Are there communication protocols in place to ensure the smooth flow of information and knowledge between vendor and client teams?
- Are there adequate intellectual property protection and security measures in place to oversee the movement and use of assets from client to the vendor?
- Is there a contingency plan to act as a backup protocol if things go off track?
- Are all of the above issues documented in a transition plan?
- Can the transition plan be used independent of the person or team that created it? Is it prepared adequately enough for all involved members to put it into practice?

8 Managing the relationship

After the transition stage, the outsourcing relationship will reach a stage of normality. During this normality stage you need to focus on managing the outsourcing relationship. However, managing the relationship during the stage of normality is not the same as when it is going through the stages of project initiation or transition. The initiation and transition stages require constant and diligent human intervention. This is because the project is in its formative period and requires a great deal of care and attention. Once the outsourcing project reaches a state of normality, the focus should be on moving from direct human intervention or supervision towards a more routine and automated governance process. This is the crux of how a successful outsourcing relationship is defined. Put another way, if the client has to constantly supervise the vendor and expel valuable resources in the management of the relationship, the outsourcing project may not yield any benefits. On the other hand, if the client can monitor the state of the outsourcing project in an efficient and effective manner, the outsourcing project is said to be successful.

Managing the relationship calls for improving upon the foundation laid down during the initiation and transition stages. The focus is on using this foundation to begin structuring the processes of relationship management, while also, we would hope, automating some of the management functions. Consider the case of issue resolution. It is conceivable that during the transition stage, the client and vendor may not have a perfect and well-oiled issue resolution process in place.

Issues that arise will need to be dealt with as they surface, in an ad-hoc and emergent fashion. However, during the normality stage, the organization can devise an automated information system to track issues, route them to the right personnel, store issue resolutions and even generate reports for management. Devising the information system will help increase the effectiveness and efficiency of how issues are resolved, thereby requiring less direct human intervention.

Relationship management includes continuous monitoring of the outsourcing engagement to ensure that expected levels of operation are being met, and also conducting routine audits on the processes. Danger signals that the outsourcing relationship is not progressing well include instances when formal measures of success are not being met, targets are being missed and the vendor seems concerned, the vendor is not speaking to the designated authorities and is finding other channels and avenues into the organization, internal staff are being lured away to work with the vendor, internal hostility towards the vendor is increasing, customer satisfaction is decreasing, the vendor is being revenue-centric instead of quality-focused. The point of good relationship management is to avoid these issues by picking up weak signals to potentially large problems early on, so that they can be dealt with straight away and bigger problems can be avoided.

There are several matters to pay attention to in the management of the relationship. We will begin by highlighting the five major areas – work administration, communication management, knowledge management, personnel management and financial management (see Figure 8.1).

Work administration

One of your most critical tasks in an outsourcing engagement is ensuring that the work that has been undertaken gets done. This task involves tracking work assignments, deliverables and resource consumption and ensuring that the overall project time line is being met. Work administration is similar in many ways to conducting the familiar task of project management. You must ensure that work assignments are being completed on time. This is especially important when you have interdependent tasks and in areas where you have not

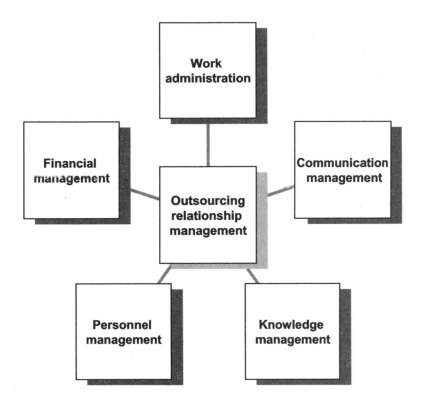

Figure 8.1 Elements of outsourcing relationship management

planned for any slack. Failure to get tasks done on time could affect the overall project schedule and the overall resource estimates of the project. Much of work administration is common to most executives, as they are routinely involved in project management. However, in the context of outsourcing, there are several singularities that demand your attention.

First you need to look at resource consumption, and roles and responsibilities management. In the SOW you have documented who is going to do what, when it is going to be done and how it is going to be done. The vendor carries out most of the work but to enable the vendor to do this work, the client naturally uses some of its resources to transfer knowledge to the vendor, such as contact people in case of systemic questions regarding the work. Without adequate client involvement in the outsourcing project, it will be very difficult for the vendor to execute its task. Here you need to be careful. In outsourcing projects that are going bad, vendors may try to upload work to client personnel. This will involve increasing the commitment of your staff to the outsourcing project beyond what is stated in the SOW. This normally begins with the vendor asking your staff to do minor additional or incremental tasks other than those specified in the SOW. If your personnel oblige, the vendor may ask for more and more. This kind of behavior needs to be nipped in the bud. Your organization will not get returns on its outsourcing efforts if it is still involved in the intricate details of the work that has been sourced out. It is important to inform the members of your outsourcing team adequately about what their roles are and what is expected from them. They should also be told to check with higher-level supervisory personnel if they are being asked to do things outside these bounds. Unless these issues are managed and dealt with in a straightforward manner promptly, the execution of tasks will become chaotic. It is foreseeable that during the initial stages of the outsourcing project personnel from the client and vendor organizations will have to make accommodations and go the extra mile to get the outsourcing project started. This ad-hoc behavior, however, needs to come to an end in the relationship management phase.

The second matter that needs careful monitoring in the outsourcing work is the evaluation of deliverables. Deliverables are critical outputs of the outsourcing project and must be given their due attention. Of special importance is the evaluation of deliverables for adherence to quality standards. It is critical that you have a team in place to evaluate the deliverables from the vendor. This team needs to pay extra attention during the initial phases of the relationship, so that errors and variances from the accepted quality standards can be addressed directly and corrections can be made. Most of the time, if you catch errors straight away and make the appropriate interventions, the project can still be successful as there is minimal resource wastage or re-work required. In contrast, if errors are caught later, after the project has passed several milestones, the cost of re-work and fixes will be severe and can jeopardize the entire project.

When devising the quality plan, be sure to take a 'big picture' view by including the quality requirements and goals, the metrics and methodologies, the tools and processes, the deliverables and artifacts, and the audits and inspections. For the purposes of the quality plan, deliverables subject to audit include planning documents, defect records and reports, and records of inspection points and reviews. You will also want to maintain the report of lessons learnt, including root-cause analysis and failure cost, as well as the project's time-reporting records, records of change and traceability records.

So how do you determine the quality of a project? You can start by applying key quality measures, such as customer satisfaction and the number of defects and their origins. Next, examine the ratio of defective and defect-free deliverables and the defect removal efficiency. Taking this one step further, consider the severity level of the defects. Finally, take into account the cost of quality and defect repairs, as well as defect complexity. In much the same way, you can also measure productivity. Begin with measures for project size, schedule and cost. Continue by examining maintenance and support measures, as well as measures for indirect cost, scope change, processes and tools. Also take a look at infrastructure efficiency and finally staff capabilities, both before and after training.

The third matter that needs your attention is ensuring that the work is being done in adherence to the operating principles outlined in the contract. Client and vendor organizations must understand the policies that they have to follow. In some situations, the vendor may be required to follow the client's procedures and policies. These generally deal with subjects such as intellectual property protection or security protocols. It is important not to fall prey to 'the-ends-justify-the-means' thinking. A vendor that is constantly violating the agreed operating principles needs to be challenged and remedies need to be taken. Remember that outsourcing involves a great deal of trust between the vendor and client organizations and a large part of building this trust is ensuring that neither party violates the principles that have been agreed upon.

Communication management

Information transfer between client and vendor is of utmost importance for successful completion of the outsourcing project. We discussed communication management in the previous chapter. However, communication management during the initial stages of the project is disorganized and seldom goes as planned. This is only to be expected, as both the client and vendor need time to adjust to the communication protocol. As the relationship moves into a stage of normality, the focus should be on trying to systematize the communication of information. One of the key elements is to increase the role played by IT in communications.

IT can play a major role in helping with the communication of information. Two kinds of information in particular concern client organizations – information about the project and information from the vendor. The former deals with issues such as how the project is progressing, whether milestones are being met or the sterling amount of costs. This information is fairly structured and can be handled with ease using traditional information-reporting tools.

An organization should always look for tools that help them simplify management of the governance process. As an example, it could have intranet portals modeled to form a 'dynamic dashboard', based on a car dashboard that gives all the vital information needed at a glance while driving. The dynamic dashboard would be a web page that provides managers with vital information about how things are progressing in the project on, say, a daily basis. It would provide executive status reports on all key aspects of the outsourcing arrangement, such as service-level performance and other performance measurements. Similarly, financial information and reporting tools give flexibility to users in picking suitable reports for their specific organization's requirements.

Why use governance tools? The advantages are many. For example, they can reduce the cost and overhead associated with the governing process. Also, they can help the organization achieve continuous improvement in the quality of performance and in satisfaction to end-users. When used effectively, these tools can help maintain the outsourcing vision and mission alignment with business goals. In addition, they can be instrumental in identifying issues like performance, quality and resource utilization. In short, these tools can help organizations improve their overall payback from outsourcing investments.

For the second kind of information, ie information from the vendor, executives cannot and should not eliminate face-to-face discussions. These must happen on a regular basis so that members from both teams can work together. However, through the use of IT, such as the use of extranets, ie intranets that can be jointly accessed between clients and vendors, organizations can make the information flow smoother.

Moreover, good e-mail protocols can be set up to ensure that information requests are routed to the right representatives from each organization. One of the problems that commonly occur in communication between individuals from two organizations is blanket e-mails. This is where one representative from either the client or the vendor organization sends an e-mail to the entire team in the other organization. In most cases, these e-mails never draw a response due to the 'bystander effect' – ie each member of the other team will think that his or her colleague will reply to the e-mail and in the end no one does.

Training and education are critical to ensure that e-mails are sent appropriately, with the right headers, to the right people and are written in an appropriate manner. It is very important to train employees on what can and cannot be written in an e-mail. E-mails have been used as evidence in legal proceedings and the company is, after all, liable for any statement or commitment made in an e-mail by any employee. Both the client's and the vendor's employees need to be strongly aware that everything written in an e-mail could be seen by people other than the recipient, so if someone is unsure about the public nature of the material, it is probably not a good idea to document it in an e-mail.

Knowledge management

During the course of an outsourcing project you are bound to gain new knowledge and experiences. This can be knowledge about the vendor, the outsourcing process and the project and can even be knowledge about your business. The various kinds of knowledge need to be leveraged in order to improve the outsourcing project, the outsourcing process and consequently even improve your business. In Chapter 10 we will discuss knowledge management in detail. For now it is important to note that there is a plan in place for knowledge assessment, transfer, retention and development, and follow up to ensure that all project participants are familiar with the latest technologies and techniques. Knowledge management involves sharing of best practices, ideas, innovations and process improvements with staff in the client organization and also between the client and the vendor organizations. This can be facilitated by having routine meetings of all staff involved in the outsourcing effort and also through the setting up of corporate repositories where employees can post their ideas, ask questions and receive answers.

Personnel management

An organization must also be clear on how it manages the various personnel involved in the outsourcing project. We suggest segmenting these project members into different teams – the executive team, the standing operational team, the committees and the special-purpose team. Each team will have a different role in overseeing the success of the outsourcing project. An outsourcing project may be faced with strategic and operational issues. Strategic issues in governance of outsourcing initiatives are high-level concerns such as financial status, organizational changes and evaluation of the overall engagement. Tactical issues are short-term and smaller in scope. They are more about immediate deliverables, risks and action items and ideally these issues should feed up, at the aggregate level, to the strategic issues. Different personnel should be responsible for different issues.

First, the organization will need a senior-level executive team that is responsible for strategic planning and development, as well as outlining the mission and vision of the governance unit. Second, it needs a standing operational team that is responsible for overseeing the day-to-day functioning and performance of the outsourcing engagement. Third, special-purpose or 'tiger teams' will be assembled to deal with critical issues as they arise. For example, if the project is going off track due to a huge backlog of work, a tiger team can be assembled to help the project out for a limited time by taking on some of the work. Finally, there will be committees that oversee various aspects of the outsourcing project, such as a committee for financial matters or for quality matters.

Each team must work with the others in concert. The advantage of having multiple teams is that this clearly separates roles and responsibilities. Moreover, there should be quicker resolution of issues and better management of the outsourcing project due to improved handling of issues and information.

Financial management

Most outsourcing agreements will involve routine and periodic payments to the vendor during the duration of the project. Financial management therefore becomes a critical issue. As money is transacted between the vendor and client, there are a few important points to bear in mind. First, if the contract was prepared adequately, it will clearly identify when monies should be paid and upon completion of which milestones. Hence, the first step for the client is to ensure that the milestones have been met. Simply because six months have transpired since the vendor took over the project does not mean that the client needs to pay out! In cases where deliverables have not been met, the client may have legal recourses to hold back some or all of the payments. These need to be enforced, so that the vendor improves its performance and gets back on track. Obviously, the severity of the issue needs to be considered. It will not be wise to hold back payments for small or insignificant issues; doing so could cause resentment and erode the trust between the vendor and the client. In cases where the client organization decides to hold back payments, there must be a discussion between the client's and the vendor's senior-level executives. This meeting should be informative and constructive, where the client should clearly explain why the payment is being withheld and under what circumstances will it be ready to release the payment. Likewise, the vendor should lay the foundation for an improved process for completing the work. The critical factor to remember here is that of equity – equity in terms of penalties for not completing the work and equity in how the partners treat each other. Both the vendor and client organizations would have invested significant resources to get where they are in the business relationship and hence must make the effort to work constructively.

In the case of utility-based and cost-plus contracts, it is also very important to get clear financial or accounting information from the vendor. In utility-based contracts, the vendor must provide the client with usage information. This information should be somewhat like a telephone bill. It must detail when the service was used, by whom, for how long and if it was used within the authorized bounds. In cost-plus contracts, the vendor must be able to defend its expense sheet clearly and provide proof when needed. It will not be wise to take round numbers and make out checks. The client must demand accurate accounting from the vendor and use such information as the basis for payments.

Finally, in financial management you must pay close and constant attention to the budget for your outsourcing project. Is the project becoming more expensive than you estimated? Once again, this is an area where you need to be particularly cautious in the early stages. Cost and resources estimates need to be monitored closely and regularly. Cases where there are serious deviations from what was projected – interventions in the form of revised estimates, meetings with the vendor, realigning the project, or all of these – need to be taken care of immediately. You must obviously try to eliminate the escalation of resource commitments beyond what was originally estimated. However, in case resource costs do escalate, you must remember not to fall prey to the sunk cost trap, where costs spent to date on a failed project only increase with the continuance of the project. Hence, you should not be thinking along the lines, 'But we've already spent X amount, so let's continue with it ...'. Instead you should think, 'Okay, so we've already spent X. Let's just pull the plug on it and not make it X + 1'.

Conclusion and checklist

In this chapter we have covered how to manage the relationship after it has passed through the project initiation and transition stages. The focus on relationship management should be to strengthen and build on the foundation laid down during the initial stages of the project. Use the following questions as a checklist:

- Is there a sound work administration program in place?
- Are there methods to catch issues at an early stage and manage them?
- Is there an adequate communication management program in place?
- Have you incorporated IT solutions to improve the effectiveness and efficiency of information transfer?
- Is there a knowledge management program in place?
- Have you segmented and clearly defined the roles of personnel involved in the outsourcing project?
- Do you have adequate controls over the financial management?

9 Continuing, modifying or terminating the arrangement

Getting the relationship management in order is only the start of the relationship, not the end. As you continue with the relationship there will be times when you must pause and evaluate the performance of the outsourcing vendor, the net gains from the relationship and how these fit with your current business needs and the realities of the marketplace.

No outsourcing relationship is smooth sailing and eventless, however much you may want it to be. Outsourcing relationships are fraught with events that require management attention. Some of these events may be considered minor and non-critical, while others are major and very serious. Up to now we have discussed how to address operational issues that arise during the outsourcing life cycle, such as communication with the vendors and poor understanding about requirements. In this chapter, we take a look at some of the *major* issues that might surface in the outsourcing engagement, serious enough to warrant management attention about deciding whether to continue or modify your existing outsourcing arrangement or even terminate it. Some examples of major events include the end of the initial probationary period, changes to your business (such as mergers and acquisitions or change in product and service offerings), changes to the vendor's business and external events such as political turmoil in the vendor's home country. The focus of this chapter will be to outline factors you must consider when making the decision to continue, modify or terminate your existing outsourcing arrangement.

We will begin by discussing the arguments you must consider when deciding whether you want to continue with the existing outsourcing agreement. Next, we talk about common events that call for you to pause and evaluate your existing outsourcing agreement, followed by a discussion on how to choose between modification and exit strategies. We conclude the chapter by examining common errors executives make when faced with the decision about whether they should modify or terminate the agreement.

The argument for continuing

Not all outsourcing relationships have to be modified or terminated. Actually, if you have built the right relationship, you would expect it to continue undisturbed until the contract termination date. When do you continue an existing agreement? The simple answer is: when you do not witness changes in your business that require a modification to the existing contract, when the vendor has been delivering at the agreed service levels and when there are no drastic changes in the environment that even question the viability of the relationship. In short, when there is no event calling for an evaluation of the existing outsourcing agreement. Events justifying an evaluation are discussed in the following section.

Continuing with an existing outsourcing relationship still requires you to stop and evaluate where you were before the outsourcing agreement, where you are now and where you want to go in future. If you can see the link between where you are currently and where you want to go, and you feel comfortable that the existing relationship will help you bridge the gap, you should stick with it.

There are several reasons that make continuing an existing agreement a superior choice. First, you don't need to reinvest time and effort in all the preceding stages of outsourcing, especially in the context of finding a new vendor. Second, staying with the existing vendor helps you avoid the burden of acquainting a new vendor with the specifics of your business. This is no small matter, as getting a new vendor up and running to meet your business challenges requires commitment of resources to an initial learning period that is normally expensive. Third, sticking with the existing contract avoids disruption to work practices and, most important, disruptions to your customers.

Unless the transition between outsourcing vendors is smooth, which it seldom is, customers will be affected. It is in an organization's best interest to minimize such disruptions. After all, customers don't care about what is going on inside your organization, as long as you deliver the product and/or service that meets their expectations.

Given these arguments for sticking with the existing contract, we must also acknowledge that critical events may arise, which call for you to consider modification or termination of the existing contract. Consider the following case in point. In early 2004, J P Morgan Chase & Co acquired Bank One in a US \$58 billion merger. The merger is expected to generate US \$2.2 billion in pre-tax cost savings over a three-year period. The two financial institutions had taken different approaches towards the management of IT. In 2002, J P Morgan Chase & Co had signed a seven-year, US \$5 billion outsourcing contract with IBM. The agreement involved transferring data-processing infrastructure, IT workers and contractors to IBM. Moreover, rather than be saddled with the large fixed costs of maintaining IT assets, J P Morgan Chase & Co purchased computing capacity as needed from IBM. On the contrary, Bank One had brought back most of its IT operations in-house. The event of the merger signaled a need for J P Morgan Chase & Co to rethink the current IT outsourcing strategy, as its new business realities made the existing outsourcing agreement obsolete in terms of fit for business needs and value.

Events that call for evaluation

We can segment into three categories events that call for the client to evaluate the outsourcing agreement (see Figure 9.1):

- internal events;
- external events;
- changes to the vendor's business.

Internal events

Businesses that do not change normally become extinct, as they cannot adapt to their environment. Embracing change is an essential part of surviving and thriving in a dynamic business landscape. While change

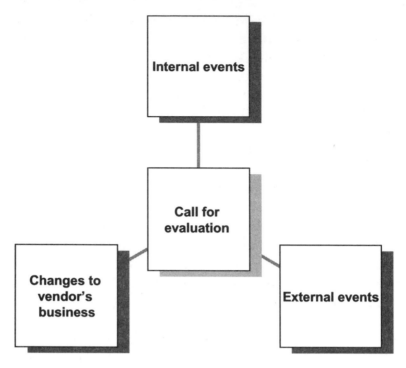

Figure 9.1 Events that call for evaluation

is essential for business success, change is also an event that may cause disruptions to existing business relationships. Outsourcing agreements are no exception. Of the many changes that an organization may face, the most serious ones that affect outsourcing include:

- changes to the composition of the business;
- changes to the core competencies of the business;
- changes to products and/or services;
- changes in stakeholder expectations.

Changes to the composition of the business include the additions, deletions or modifications to the organizational structure. Most commonly this occurs when an organization forges new alliances, modifies or terminates existing ones and when it goes in for mergers and acquisitions. Entering into a new alliance or acquiring an organization may make the existing outsourcing arrangement redundant or obsolete. For instance, if a technology organization acquires an incumbent firm who has expertise in a particular domain, its existing alliances with business partners in this domain may become redundant. In another case, if an organization acquires new customers and business partners, its outsourcing agreement may need to be revised to accommodate the new business.

Changes to the composition of a business are structural in nature. Changes to the core competencies of an organization can also occur. Core competencies are an organization's 'bread and butter' – the revenue drivers. For Dell Computers it is the ability to manage its supply chain systems, for Microsoft it is the ability to build innovative software and for Boeing it is transitioning from a manufacturer to a systems integrator of military and commercial aircraft. If an organization decides to abandon an area of core competency in favor of new ones, changes will be required in its internal structure and work practices. Abandoning existing competencies will result in a restructuring of existing relationships, as there will a shift in how funds are spent in the organization. For instance, if a PC manufacturer decides to abandon the production of desktop computers in favor of a more upmarket and larger selection of notebooks, resources are going to be diverted from the PCs to the notebooks. Since hardware specifications differ between PCs and notebooks, chances are that many of the organizations' current agreements with PC component manufacturers will need to be redesigned. Changes to core competencies may manifest themselves in changes to products and services. Changes to an organization's deliverables may also affect outsourcing agreements. A simple example is the case of digitization of products and services via the internet. Today, many of us still like to read books and buy CDs; tomorrow much of this material will be available at a significantly lower rate on the internet, resulting in lower traffic in terms of shipping volumes. It is conceivable that as more products get digitized and the sophistication of internet connectivity continues to grow, most notably in greater bandwidth, we will begin to see changes to current outsourcing arrangements involving logistics.

Finally, organizations must also be aware of changes in stakeholder expectations, as they affect how outsourcing is perceived within and outside the organization. Companies such as Dell Computers were forced to bring back offshore call centers after a slew of customer (stakeholder) complaints regarding the level of customer service. Customers of a business are also sometimes its employees. Political backlash from the outsourcing of jobs can affect the employee morale of the organization and may hurt organizational performance. In addition, if stakeholders within organizations, such as project managers, perceive outsourcing agreements as falling short of stated expectation and not resulting in perceived benefits, such agreements may become unfavorable and may be a difficult sell to others in the organization.

External events

A major concern about changes in the environment is political turmoil or unrest in the vendor's country of operations. In fact, the location of your vendors is as important an issue as the location of your office. If there is political unrest in the service provider's geographical location, the vendor's business will be compromised. This, in turn, will directly affect how your business is conducted. Not surprisingly, today, when it comes to information systems outsourcing, many up-and-coming vendors in the outsourcing world have to deal with issues of political instability. For example, if organizations have to choose between outsourcing to India or Pakistan, assuming both have the same level of workforce, cost structures and infrastructure, most would choose India over Pakistan. The key reason is that India has greater political stability.

In addition to political unrest, clients must also be cognizant of economic changes in the outsourcing vendor's location. For example, currently India, the dominant IT outsourcing offshore market, is witnessing a rise in IT worker wages. Hence previously estimated cost savings that made India a lucrative market space need to be revised. This is not to say that India cannot be a dominant player in the software offshore business; however, its competency in the area of innovating software, superior quality, better project management and other such attributes will determine its future, not its ability to sustain lower software development cost. Economic conditions go beyond rises in wages to include other issues such as changes to local business laws, foreign policies and currency exchange rates. All of these affect outsourcing contracts in some fashion. The seriousness of the impact determines whether or not an organization needs to modify the outsourcing agreement.

The next important factor in the business environment is innovation. All disciplines are witnessing high rates of innovation. Much of innovation disrupts existing work practice. An innovation in one area usually causes another area to become obsolete. Hence, if an organization is in a long-term contract and an innovation takes a hold in the market that affects the business, the value of the outsourcing contract may be in jeopardy. Innovations can change the definition of what should be fixed versus variable costs in an industry. Today, we are seeing an interest in the concept of on-demand computing. As the name implies, this involves renting computing power as needed to meet emergent needs. Rather than trying to forecast computing needs and purchasing the requisite hardware and software, organizations are moving to this more flexible model. This alleviates the need to have a large fixed cost of computer hardware. On-demand computing is affecting the way organizations purchase computing power and many organizations are currently in the process of revising or terminating their current plans with information system vendors in favor of a more flexible approach.

The final factors that may entice an organization to evaluate its outsourcing plans are political backlash, legal sanctions and national trade policies. There have been some recent cases of outsourcing backlashes. Public opinion in the developed nations may be violently against outsourcing. Public opinion backlashes can manifest themselves in many ways. In June 2002, the Organization for the Rights of American Workers (Toraw), a group of displaced, angry US workers made redundant by Connecticut (USA) insurance and financial services companies held a two-day demonstration outside the Strategic Outsourcing Conference at the Waldorf Astoria hotel in New York City. The same month, other redundant workers demonstrated outside an outsourcing conference at the Hynes Convention Center in Boston. Public opinion is important for organizations to consider as it may affect how consumers perceive organizations' products and services. In some cases, negative public opinion can also lead to lobbying for trade and employment restrictions in the form of laws. Governments may step in to protect their working class and may take steps to curtail the amount and type of outsourcing projects an organization may consider.

It is our contention that emotional stances against (or even for) outsourcing are a passing fad. The economics of outsourcing, especially offshore outsourcing, is too good an opportunity to pass up. Moreover, in a global society, and where open and free markets dominate, it is naive to think that one can control the movement of labor or capital with laws. However, we do realize the seriousness of political and public opinion backlashes on outsourcing. It is hence important for an organization to use these opportunities to evaluate its existing outsourcing strategy. The focus should be to identify how outsourcing is perceived by their internal and external stakeholders, what can be done to minimize negative opinions and how outsourcing can be positioned in a positive light. We do not recommend that an organization simply cut back outsourcing plans or engage in any other quick erratic reactions.

Changes to the vendor's business

An organization with outsourcing arrangements must constantly evaluate the vendor's financial and market viability. Failure to do so will leave it unprepared to deal with contingencies such as a vendor going bankrupt. In 2000, when one of us was involved with a software manufacturer, a vendor closed down its business without fair warning. Companies that relied on the vendor were given 48 hours to move their data off the vendor's server before the creditors came to collect. Situations such as this can be avoided if organizations routinely evaluate their vendors' financial and market viability. This routine evaluation will give a sense of the longevity of a vendor organization and its consequent ability to keep up with commitments. When a vendor organization starts losing control over its market share, this may indicate that the vendor is heading for hard times. Such indications suggest that it may be time for a client organization to consider partnering with a new vendor. It is therefore essential that your organization is prepared to modify or terminate the contract if you suspect a vendor's market and financial viability.

Another serious issue in terms of changes to the vendor's business is the change of senior executives. Senior executives set the direction, vision and tone of the organization. As new senior executives replace old ones, there might be changes in the organization's direction and focus. If these affect your outsourcing relationship – for example, if the new senior executive decides to abandon innovation in a domain of interest – you may want to rethink the existing outsourcing contract.

Depending on the competitive situations in the industry, you may need to revise agreements if a vendor organization chooses to ally itself with firms that you compete with or that are otherwise hostile entities. In this case, issues of intellectual capital protection and other security issues arise. For example, if a vendor collaborates with your competitor to build a system similar to the one that is being built for you, critical issues emerge, such as how you share knowledge with the vendor and how it should be protected from leakage to the competitor.

If vendors are facing legal difficulties and regulatory compliance issues, the backlash from such events could affect your business. Association with culpable vendors could have direct or indirect impact in the form of loss of brand image or brand name. In the first case, a vendor is so buried in dealing with legal issues that its performance of contract deliverable may be lacking and incomplete. In the second case, the market – and more importantly, your customers – may tend to misjudge you owing to your association with the vendor, depending on your legal situation. For instance, once it was known that Arthur Andersen was involved in unscrupulous accounting practices, many of its clients switched their auditing and tax service processes to other vendors, not because they doubted Arthur Andersen's knowledge and ability, but because they doubted its credibility. Pressures from shareholders and the market were serious enough to compel many organizations to withdraw from their auditing contracts straight away.

Modification or exit strategies

If any of the above events arise, your organization must think very seriously about how best to modify its existing outsourcing agreement. Most of the time there are two choices: modify or tweak the existing outsourcing agreement to be more appreciative of new realities; terminate the existing agreement and arrive at a new strategy. Making the right choice is a critical issue and can have serious consequences on the organization's business. Moreover, there is no general algorithm that can be used to make the decision. The following guidelines should help.

An outsourcing contract can be viewed as consisting of a fixed and a variable component. The fixed component is the standardized content of the contract and includes the traditional disclaimers, details about the vendor's business, nature of interacting with the vendor and similar details that the vendor supplies to all its clients. The variable part of the contract includes customized information reflecting your business peculiarities. Details such as the pricing, nature of service delivery, number of transactions being processed, nature of customer support, fees and similar details are all part of the variable section of the contract. The vendor will customize the variable component for each client. For example, a small business client may not have as many transactions as a Fortune 100 company and hence may demand a different pricing schedule. Normally, the contract will state that changing either the fixed or variable components of the contract will call for a modification or exit strategy. After all, the contract is the explicit documented definition of the current outsourcing relationship.

Modification of the existing contract is appropriate when external events indicate a need for change in the variables or customizable components of an existing agreement. For instance, if you need to increase the volume of transactions being processed on your vendor's IT system, it may be viable to modify the existing outsourcing contract rather than trying to find a new vendor.

Exit strategies are to be considered when your requirements go beyond tweaking the variables. An exit strategy requires a greater deal of time and effort, hence this option must be used with the strictest caution. In the previous section we have discussed events that demand an evaluation of the current contract. These events – major changes to your business, major changes in the business environment or major changes to the vendor's business –may also call for an exit strategy. Take the following examples. Entering into a merger and/or acquisition may require you to rethink the way your IT work is conducted. Long-term political unrest in the vendor's location make an exit strategy imperative, because no matter how much discount the vendor is ready is provide, ie changing the variables to offer a better deal, terminating the contract will be better in the long term and lower the risk to your organization's operations. Indications about the vendor's declining financial health may cause concern about its ability to continue operating in the foreseeable future, so you may want to move your business elsewhere. In short, events that require you to change the standardized or fixed aspects of a contract normally call for terminating the existing agreement and searching for a new business partner where the fixed component is a better match for your needs.

Common decision errors

Getting caught in the sunk cost trap
Falling for 'a fantastic deal'
Failing to recognize a good thing when you have one
Maintaining the right number of vendors
Forgetting that 'a stitch in time saves nine'

Common decision errors

Some of the common errors made by organizations when contemplating the decision to modify or exit an outsourcing decision are discussed below.

Getting caught in the sunk cost trap

Sunk cost represents the expenditure an organization has incurred to date. Most organizations take sunk cost into account when trying to chart out a future course of action. This is a futile effort, as by its very name, sunk cost represents the funds that have sunk into oblivion, without hope of return or recovery. Organizations need to wipe the slate clean and begin to think in new and open terms when making a modification or exit strategy. Taking sunk cost into account will almost always result in a 'no new action' decision, as executives tends to feel, 'We have already spent X amount, so why not stick with it and carry on?' Sticking with a failed course of action is sure to cost the organization greater resources than it has spent to date. Sunk cost must not be taken into the accounting picture when charting a future course; instead the organization must start afresh by evaluating the existing contract and seeking possible alternatives that will deliver future value.

Falling for 'a fantastic deal'

The current marketplace is closely and fiercely competitive. Hence, when a client organization indicates that it is willing to terminate an existing agreement, the market takes notice. No sooner is such information released to the market than the organization will be bombarded with 'a fantastic deal' from numerous vendors wanting to lure the client. What happens here is simple; the unprepared client will not know how to deal with the influx of information. This is especially true if the client has just terminated an outsourcing contract on a bad note. In this case, any new proposal will seem better than the last one and there is a tendency to get sloppy in evaluating the incoming information. Most of the time, initial excitement will blind the client to the nitty-gritty, also commonly known as the hidden clauses in the contract. Lack of proper evaluation here will come back to haunt the organization in the long run.

Failing to recognize a good thing

'The grass is always greener on the other side' – until you cross over to the other side! All too often, client organizations are continuously bombarded with claims by vendors that make them question their existing agreements. If handled properly, such incoming information can keep a client on its toes and help in good governance of the outsourcing relationship. However, there is also a tendency to get irritated or frustrated with the existing relationship for miniscule reasons. Take the issue of the cost. Most vendors will promise to lower the cost of the existing contract and help improve the bottom line, but how many will deliver? Additionally, switching to a new vendor will require an organization to commit to an initial learning period, wherein the vendor acquaints itself with the client's business. Hence, no cost savings are going to be realized immediately. Moreover, switching to a new vendor will require the client to re-dedicate people and resources for project transition and other early governance issues. These costs may be worthwhile to bear if the vendor has been performing miserably and there is a dire need to get out of the existing contract. For miniscule cost savings, however, such efforts are not warranted because any cost savings will be buried within these expenses. An organization must recognize the value of a good relationship and not try to scrimp and save excessively in an ongoing relationship.

Maintaining the right number of vendors

Most organizations struggle with balancing risks between having multiple outsourcing partners and having a single one. This is an important issue and you must consider it seriously. On the one hand, with multiple outsourcing partners an organization has the burden of coordinating activities among them. Doing so is not free of cost implications and unless the outsourcing vendors are working on very specific components that are largely independent of one another, the organization is going to have trouble coordinating activities. This practice is common in the US Defense Department and other highly sensitive organizations. Here, each outsourcing vendor is given a portion of the entire project to work on, without knowing the complete details of the project. Only the organization holds the overall framework and it plays the role of an integrator who combines the various pieces.

On the other hand, an organization can have one outsourcing vendor who is responsible for the entire project. Here, much of the coordination activity is lowered and is borne by the vendor. However, this is not a panacea. By going with one outsourcing vendor, an organization basically 'puts all its eggs in one basket'. Rather than dividing the risks of the outsourcing project among multiple vendors, it has to rely exclusively on one. There is also a greater burden in terms of continuance, modification or exit strategies here. If a client decides to continue with the sole vendor, then the vendor begins to increase the role it plays in the client organization and might be in an advantageous position. This would make it possible for the vendor to take the organization hostage or make it difficult for it to modify the contract to one that is beneficial to it. If the client decides to exit, then it has a higher burden in terms of finding a new vendor who is qualified or available to take on a large project instead of helping out with a small component, as would be the case in the strategy of using multiple vendors.

Your organization must therefore make a very carefully calculated decision about which option it plans to use, with full recognition of the costs and benefits of its decision. There is no one strategy that will work for every organization or for every project. Issues of trust in the vendor, past relationships with the vendor and availability of alternative choices all need to be accounted for when making this decision.

Forgetting that 'a stitch in time saves nine'

In the final analysis, all organizations want to choose a vendor that is reliable, easy to work with and beneficial to their business. Consequently, it is important that they pay attention to the relationship with the vendor from the onset and avoid reaching a point where exit strategies become essential. Problems with the governance of the relationship must be attended to in their early stages rather than having them build up to an unmanageable stage. Issues dealt with at an early stage can result in an improved relationship with the vendor and will also cost the organization less in terms of resources. Allowing issues to escalate will almost surely lead to a termination of the contract, which is an expensive proposition. Modifications to a contract are normally a better proposition, as long as both parties are going to gain from the changes. It is therefore easier, and often better, to modify an existing contract rather than leave one halfway and try to find a replacement for the vendor and a new contract. Modifications to a contract can include issues that arise during a relationship or due to changes in the business needs of the organization. Exiting an alliance is difficult not only in terms of the economic and financial ramifications, but more so in terms of the disruption to the organization's business. Of course, if there are serious changes in your business that require an exit strategy, you must go with it, but at least you will end the association on pleasant terms. In the future, should you need the services of the vendor, structuring a deal will be a lot easier.

The exit strategy

As we discussed in Chapter 6, it is important to have an exit strategy when signing the contract. Just in case you missed that point, here is a recap. Unless you have an exit strategy that is planned for and thought through up front, you will be a hostage in the outsourcing relationship. The exit strategy devised during the negotiation and contracting phases of the outsourcing life cycle needs to be continuously revised as the relationship management process continues, because there will be new information that is made available in the course of the ongoing relationship that will call for revising the exit strategy.

A good exit strategy will be evaluated constantly and must have definite answers to the following questions: What are the steps your organization should take to ensure that your processes can continue without interruptions should your vendor (1) go out of business? (2) suffer from temporary interruptions of service provision?

Having an answer to the first question makes you recognize the fact that all vendors have weaknesses and sometimes these weaknesses may overpower the organization leading to some sort of collapse. To you, the client organization, it is really immaterial *why* the vendor could fail – whether it may close down because of a large lawsuit or be hit by a natural disaster. The point to focus on is how to move out of the relationship and continue operations in a short period of time. Most organizations normally have a window of 24–48 hours to move operations to avoid major disruptions to their business; after this period it becomes a constant game of catching up. Just imagine the following. Suppose a company like amazon.com had a temporary lapse of their servers and assume that they did not have an adequate backup procedure in place, resulting in a week's wait before operations could be resumed. The chances are high that they will never reopen their business as the losses they incur in terms of revenue, market share and brand name will be simply overwhelming.

Having an answer to the second question is important, and will be different from your first answer. The second answer calls for a temporary measure, where you are looking for an immediate short-term solution. Organizations normally enter utility-based contracts to secure a temporary solution. In these contracts, the organization negotiates a deal with a third party to use resources for a temporary period. The organization normally has to pay a retainer or base fee to keep the contract open, plus an additional fee when the organization actually exercises its option to use the resources on a temporary basis. As indicated in Chapter 6, utility contracts are good for short-term assignments and hence should not be used as long-term alternatives for interruptions in the vendor's service provision. This is why it is important that an organization have an answer to each question in terms of an exit strategy to cover both the long term and the short term.

An exit strategy must be constantly evaluated, re-evaluated and modified to keep up with changes in the outsourcing relationship. There is no use having an exit strategy that is outdated – that is like having an insurance policy but not paying your premiums – if a fire burns down the building, there will be no reimbursement. The final point regarding the exit strategy is to ensure that one is not unduly cost-conscious when putting it in place. Cutting corners when putting an exit strategy in place will come back to haunt the organization when a disaster does materialize.

Conclusion and checklist

In this chapter, we have discussed the final stage in the outsourcing life cycle. The experienced executive will be aware of the various events outlined in this chapter and of their effects on the current outsourcing arrangement. Modifications and terminations of current outsourcing agreements require executives to restart the life-cycle process. You will need to reassess the organization in terms of its readiness for outsourcing. You may need to dispense with outsourcing and move the work in-house only because, since the start of the outsourcing engagements, there have been significant changes in the business that demand such a decision. If you decide that you still want to outsource the activity but have terminated the existing agreement, you will need to conduct a new search for a vendor, renegotiate a favorable contract and start the governance process again.

It is in your organization's best interest to play the devil's advocate when routinely evaluating the outsourcing agreement. Questions that should be raised include:

- What happens if our production capacity increases? Will our vendor be able to scale up?
- What happens if our vendor closes down tomorrow? Do we have a backup plan or exit strategy?
- What happens if we discontinue product lines? Is the outsourcing arrangement flexible enough for the change?

Questions such as these force you to think in terms of probability scenarios and develop plans around them. Waiting for an event to materialize before starting to plan is a cardinal sin. If you do not plan in advance for events you are at best only able to be reactive. Here you must pay attention to the following checklist:

- Do you understand changes in the external environment that might affect the viability of your outsourcing strategy?
- Do you understand internal changes in your business that call for realignment of the existing outsourcing strategy?
- Do you understand changes in your vendor's business strategy that may require you to rethink the existing outsourcing relationship?

- Do you understand the pros and cons of continuing an outsourcing relationship?
- Is there a viable exit strategy in place?

This chapter concludes our discussion of the outsourcing life cycle. In the next chapter, we will examine how an organization can repeat the process of outsourcing in an improved fashion. To do this, an organization must be successful in managing knowledge in and around outsourcing efforts so that both positive and negative experiences and lessons learnt can be used to reinforce the outsourcing process. In addition, it is important for an organization to devise appropriate metrics to evaluate the process of outsourcing and use such metrics to continuously improve the process. Finally, it is also important for an organization to mature its outsourcing life-cycle process. Maturing an outsourcing process involves both time and effort, in addition to management interventions for continuous improvement. We will discuss each of these important factors in the next chapter.

10 Back on the dance floor – repeating the process

Most organizations move through the outsourcing life cycle multiple times (Power, Desouza and Bonifazi, 2005). Some have the unfortunate experience of repeating the same mistakes over and over again, while a few others progress towards a more improved process methodology. The focus of this chapter will be to examine what it takes to improve the outsourcing experience – in particular, how to improve progression through the various stages of the outsourcing life cycle. We will do this by examining several salient concepts and issues.

First, we must acknowledge that no organization will be an expert in moving through the outsourcing life-cycle process from the very first day, just as we would not expect any of us to be an expert in writing a book when we first start (even after authoring four books, one of us is still far from being an expert!). Mistakes, surprises, errors, failures, foul-ups and blunders are all part of the trying-and-testing game. Unless executives are ready to experiment with the concept of outsourcing, they are never going to learn. Reading about outsourcing is one thing; trying to implement it in practice is quite another. By accepting the reality that in the beginning most of us are experimenters with the concept of outsourcing, we must also acknowledge that we are not perfect and that deviations from the expected trajectory *will* occur. It is by examining these deviations that we can learn how to improve the process of outsourcing and make for a better future process.

Second, the adage 'practice makes perfect' holds true for any endeavor, including outsourcing. Unless they are prepared to put their knowledge of outsourcing through routine practice, executives cannot expect to improve the process to a measure of perfection. However, one caveat needs to be addressed up front – blind practice or repeated practice of an error-prone process, will only reinforce a bad process. Hence, while practice is essential, executives must ensure that what they are practicing is actually correct. The analogy of training athletes comes to mind here. Most sports coaches spend significant amounts of time and energy to ensure that their players learn the correct playing tactics and methods. Kicking a football is a skill that improves with practice. The skill, however, has basic principles – the placement of the ball, the posture of the foot, the direction of body movement, etc – all of which need to be learnt and internalized. Failure to do so will, at best, result in the ability to kick the ball with power and vigor but with no sense of direction or placement, which at the end of the day is quite useless – after all, the team objective is to place the ball in the opponent's goal. Unless organizations are cognizant about their mistakes and have guidance on the right way to proceed towards improvement, simple repetition of the outsourcing process will do them little good.

Finally, in order to improve a process organizations must be able to measure it. Measures give indicators about how the process is performing. In doing so, they also indicate whether managerial intervention is helping improve the process. Without appropriate attention to measurement, at best organizations will only be able to make informed guesses about the state of the process – quite a futile exercise. Measuring a process, however, is not as simple as it sounds. As we will discuss in this chapter, in order to measure a process it must first be stable and non-chaotic. This in itself is an ambitious feat for organizations to achieve in terms of their outsourcing methodology.

We will now explore the above concepts in detail. We will begin by addressing the concept of knowledge management. Knowledge management as a business concept has been around since the late 1990s. Rather than covering an entire literature review of this concept, we will focus here on demonstrating its value and prominence in terms of managing outsourcing efforts. Following this, we will explore the concept of metrics. Here, we will elaborate on ways to calibrate metrics for outsourcing endeavors and management of metrics. Next, we will propose a maturity model that charts out a trajectory that an organization will progressively follow as their experience and knowledge of outsourcing methodologies increases. We will conclude the chapter by discussing the concept of a relationship management office (RMO). We envision organizations developing RMOs as centers that are accountable and responsible for managing outsourcing relationships.

Knowledge management

Knowledge is the collection of experiences, insights, hunches and skills possessed by an entity. This entity can be an individual, a group or an organization. Each of us has knowledge; some of it is common knowledge, ie insights shared by most members of society, and some of it is our unique, private knowledge. It is the private knowledge that helps us earn an income, as we are able to contribute something of value to society. Of course, the rarer and the more in demand our private knowledge, the greater is our chance of earning a higher income. Similar dynamics occur at the group and organizational levels. What makes Microsoft the best software organization in the world? The knowledge possessed by its employees and the ability of the managers of the organization to integrate and leverage such knowledge for attainment of organizational ends in an effective and efficient manner. Effective knowledge management is what makes one company better than another. There are entire textbooks and several thousand articles on the topic of knowledge management. Consequently, we will not dwell on the generalities of the concept here, but will instead hone in on its applicability to improve the management of outsourcing (Nonaka and Takeuchi, 1995; Davenport and Prusak, 1998; Desouza and Awazu, 2005a).

In the context of outsourcing, knowledge management plays a vital role in improving the outsourcing life cycle. Knowledge possessed by an organization on outsourcing can be used to differentiate it from its competitors. If an organization is successful in its ability to develop outsourcing as a strategic tool, ie to practice the art of outsourcing in an effective and efficient manner, rest assured that it will have an edge on its competitors in terms of effectiveness and efficiency of operations. The challenge for any organization is to create, store, retrieve and apply knowledge: the knowledge-management process life cycle. Let us walk through each concept.

Knowledge creation deals with eliciting best practices, experiences, skills and other relevant know-how from the employees within the organization or seeking it from sources external to the organization. No organization will be self-sufficient in all operational areas and, quite often, organizations have to rely on their business partners for valuable knowledge. Moreover, an *employee* possessing knowledge is hardly the same as the *organization* possessing it. Organizational knowledge is not the simple summation of individual know-how. In the context of outsourcing, once organizations have the basic outsourcing life cycle in operation, they must begin to create knowledge about it. Doing so will require them to seek feedback from those involved in the various stages of outsourcing, have them document their experiences, share these experiences and know-how with other organizational members and integrate or synthesize these to develop knowledge.

One of the most common ways of creating knowledge after projects is through conducting postmortem analyses (Desouza, Dingsøyr and Awazu, 2005). Conducting a postmortem, either after a milestone or at the end of a project, is crucial in order to gauge what has been learnt, what main issues were faced and what can be used to improve the work processes in future. Conducting postmortems helps to articulate tacit experiences into explicit forms, thereby enabling experiences to be better reused in the future. The main motivation is to reflect on what happened in the project in order to improve future practice, both for the individuals who have participated in the project and for the organization as a whole. The intended result of a postmortem should be learning and not project evaluation. Evaluation can lead to people not sharing experiences that they think can embarrass them. Learning through postmortems must occur at three levels – the individual, the team and the organization.

Individuals involved, ie project members, must learn from their conduct during the project. This learning will call for taking a retrospective look at how they performed key tasks, the difficulties they faced, barriers they had to overcome, mechanisms that were helpful for goal attainments and other details. The postmortem affords individuals the opportunity to receive structured feedback on their performance on the project. At the individual level, postmortems also help to identify areas of managerial or technical competencies that need to be improved for better success in future projects. For instance, an individual may realize that during the project his or her knowledge in Enterprise JAVA Beans may not have been up to par, slowing down the project. The individual could use this insight to improve his or her skills to be better prepared for future work assignments. Similarly, individuals could learn that they need to improve their managerial skills such as oral and written communications or project management skills.

For project managers, postmortems enable reflection on management approaches, styles, conventions, and their associated effectiveness in attaining project targets. For the team, a postmortem provides a venue to discuss how the collaboration and coordination were organized. Seldom is a project completed without conflicts among group members. Conflicts do not have to be major incidents; they can be disagreements over work practices, methodologies, output deliveries, etc. During the course of our research, we found that most commonly team members disagreed on the amount of testing required, the scope of reuse, process and methodology issues and communication issues. It is important that once a project is completed, team members reflect on these situations so that lessons can be drawn and mistakes can be avoided in future.

For the organization, a postmortem allows for the tacit insights from a project to be captured and made available to the rest of the organizational members. A postmortem provides an opportunity to reflect on company-wide policies, processes, strategies and models. In order to be effective for organizational-wide learning, lessons learnt will have to be decontextualized from the project at hand and be made applicable to the other activities the organization engages in. At the organizational level, we are concerned with eliciting knowledge *from* projects that can be used across current projects that are under way as well as for future projects (Desouza and Evaristo, 2005). A postmortem analysis only has value if the lessons learnt (knowledge) are used to inform future practices of project management.

Once created, knowledge storage and knowledge retrieval become critical factors that must be attended to. Failure to store knowledge for future use will result in organizations recreating the same knowledge over and over again – an economically unwise option. Knowledge needs to be made available in an explicit form before it can be stored in a physical form. Normally, this is implemented through three main procedures:

- creating reports;
- writing narratives or stories;
- composing best practices.

A report is a structured presentation of lessons learnt during a project. Reports are compiled by using predefined organizational templates. A typical report template includes an introduction with information about the project and how the postmortem was conducted, lists of issues that went well in the project as well as analyses of the most important issues, lists of issues that did not go well with accompanying analyses and finally appendices with full lists of topics that appeared in the postmortem and possibly transcripts of discussions. Reports work well for capturing knowledge from routine projects and where there is not much ambiguity in the context of transpiring events. Moreover, capturing insights using reports allows one to trace the history of problems and see if things are being fixed, root causes of problems are being addressed or if symptoms are reoccurring. Composing reports is the least cognitively challenging of the three types of documentation.

A narrative or story is the most cognitively challenging form of documentation. Through the use of narratives managers can develop learning histories. In learning histories, narratives are used to transfer experience, taking into account the importance of storytelling and myths in organizations. A learning history is created by interviewing participants in an individual project and then working on the material to create a story. Some basic principles have to be followed. A story starts with a curtain-raiser, a kernel paragraph and an exposition containing the main points of the story. The main story is presented as a jointly told tale, with the narrator's voice in one column and direct voice in another column. Usually, the main story is organized in thematic chapters with their own kernel paragraph and exposition. The story concludes with a closing section, which connects to the curtain-raiser. Stories are more detailed than reports and can therefore offer richer knowledge by providing the ability to incorporate contextual details into the plot of the story. As a result of this elaboration, stories are more difficult to comprehend than reports. They are longer and require more of the reader's cognitive resources. Moreover, due to the lack of structure and directness, a story can be analyzed in multiple ways; this equivocality leads to multiple interpretations between individuals. An individual can also have multiple interpretations of a story after reading it two or more times. A report will precisely inform the reader about the key lessons, while stories leave it up to readers to derive their own lessons learnt. Stories are not as amenable to the use of automated technologies as reports – for instance, it is difficult to run automated searches on stories, as the reader may not know the search context.

When should managers use stories and when should they use reports? If the project is unique and there have been significant peculiarities during its life cycle, it is best to capture the postmortem analysis as a story; otherwise a report will suffice. Writing a story is a more costly and time-consuming effort, hence the effort must be warranted by expected benefits – ie knowledge about the nature of the project. If resources are scarce, it is better to write the postmortem analysis as a report as it needs fewer resources. Trying to write a story with an insufficient budget will be difficult. Stories make more organizational impact than reports, leading to organization-wide discussions, debates and interpretations. Hence, they are ideal for capturing lessons of a significant magnitude. Reports, on the other hand, are more simple and humble and are apt for capturing lessons learnt on routine endeavors.

Choosing when to write a story is very important so as not to fall prey to the 'cry-wolf' syndrome by calling attention to non-significant stories. If an organization writes a story for every small novelty, stories will lose their significance in the organization. While stories are an excellent means to communicate the norms, core beliefs and values of the organization, they are less suitable for conveying rules or policies, which are more easily conveyed using reports. Stories are good at driving home moral lessons whereas reports are better suited for directly and concisely communicating operational lessons learnt.

The above guidelines will enable managers to better choose the output of postmortem analyses. Unless the right postmortem output is chosen, management will not attain the desired learning outcomes. Reports are best used to build on past efforts and can help in incremental learning efforts. Stories, on the other hand, are used to attain radical learning outcomes as they are dramatic and call for unlearning of previous behaviors. The challenge for the organization is to find the right mix of postmortem reports and stories.

Composing best practices can only take place when an organization has had sufficient time to see what works and what does not. This occurs only after an organization has reached level 5 maturity on the Outsourcing Management Maturity Model (OMMM). We will discuss the OMMM in a later section. Best practices are a composite of reports and stories. They detail the best-of-breed processes and how these should be implemented in the organization. Best practices require collating the sets of experiences on a given topic, debating them and then arriving at the final list of best practices. Only an organization that has first implemented a stable outsourcing process needs to consider this, as for all others the priority lies in first stabilizing the outsourcing process.

Best practices represent an organization's intellectual assets and hence must be protected just like other valuables (Desouza and Vanapalli, 2005). Proper security protocols need to be in place to prevent unauthorized leakage of such knowledge to competitors or to unscrupulous individuals. Moreover, it is also important to put a program in place to identify who has the rights and authority to incorporate best practices. For instance, organizations would want to train or orient managers into the concepts of the best practices before allowing them to apply them. Why is this important? Basically because, as the saying goes, 'A little knowledge is a dangerous thing'. Unless managers are trained in the specifics of best practices and understand the context and rationale behind them, they are bound to apply them incorrectly, as merely reading the document will not give them the entire picture. Having a program in place to train managers and share best practices with only those who have acquired certain level of experience enables organizations to ensure quality control in how knowledge is applied.

Knowledge application is how organizations get the returns on the investments for capturing, storing and transferring knowledge. Without application, a knowledge-management program is worthless. Applying knowledge should be made a part and parcel of the organizational culture. This can be done by building checks and balances in the outsourcing process that require a manager to question whether past knowledge is being applied. For instance, if an organization is using an automated tool for vendor assessments, it can have controls in place that ask managers if they have reviewed a certain best practice before completing the document. This will remind the manager that such knowledge exists in the organization and it is best to check it rather than risk errors.

Applying knowledge also calls for having a strong training program in place. In most organizations the 80/20 rule exists: 80 per cent of the knowledge is created by 20 per cent of the employees. Moreover, this 80 per cent of knowledge is only known to the 20 per cent, hence there will be wide discrepancies in how individual managers perform in terms of knowledge management. An organization must have training programs in place to transfer knowledge to personnel who are responsible for outsourcing efforts. Training can include both formal practices such as classroom instructions and informal methods such as having new project managers assigned to mentors.

All in all, having a viable knowledge-management program is an absolute essential in order to have an outsourcing program that continuously learns and improves itself. Just as we humans try to increase our knowledge in our domains of interest everyday, so we must allow an outsourcing program to mature and improve itself.

Metrics

Metrics to evaluate a phenomenon normally fall into two categories – process metrics and output metrics. Process metrics evaluate the steps required to move from inputs to outputs. In the case of a bakery, this involves measuring the steps required to move from kneading the flour up to the point where the baked bread is packaged and ready for sale. Output metrics are those that evaluate the finished product. Continuing with the bread analogy, output metrics would be indicators such as 'How does the bread taste?' and 'What is its texture?' and other qualitative indicators of the finished product. Output evaluations are normally made by the customers of the product or service, whereas process evaluations are conducted by the producing organization. Output metrics are more subjective and may vary highly depending on the nature of the customer answering the questions. For instance, evaluations on a bottle of wine will differ between a connoisseur of fine wines and an infrequent wine drinker. Output metrics give a sense of how those who are outside the production process view the product and whether the product meets the demands of the customer.

Measuring processes

The first step towards measuring a process is the ability to define the process. Without an adequate definition of what is being measured, organizations might be inclined to measure different things at different points in time, or different people will measure different things, as there is lack of consensus about the artifact being measured. In the context of outsourcing, organizations must be clear on the definition of the process and its various components. As outlined in this book, the outsourcing life cycle can be broken down into several components, beginning with the strategic assessment and ending with the decision to continue, modify or terminate the agreement. We suggest that managers use these stages to define the components of the outsourcing process and also outline its scope. It is essential that an organization publish a definition of each term in the outsourcing life cycle, and in doing so, clearly specifies what is included in a stage and consequently makes clear what is not included.

Once the process is defined, the second step involves articulating what attribute is being measured. For any artifact multiple items can be measured. For example, in weight training, one can measure the amount of body fat, the stamina, the muscle strength and a whole slew of other indicators of the human body. Moreover, one can use composite indicators that integrate individual indicators such as the body mass index (BMI). The BMI provides a composite score of one's physique by compiling height and weight indicators. In the case of outsourcing, organizations must be clear about what each indicator of outsourcing is measuring and how each indicator relates to other indicators. For instance, organizations must specify whether individual indicators can be combined to arrive at a composite score. It is common to measure attributes such as the time taken to complete the process and the number of critical issues that arise during the conduct of a process.

The third step involves analyzing the measures, basically answering the question: What do the indicators tell organizations? For scores to be meaningful, managers need to understand them within a given context. Context normally involves two items: history of the process and outsider information. History of the process gives indicators about how the organization is doing currently compared to how it was doing in the past. It hopes to fare better on positive indicators while lowering the numbers on negative indicators. Developing a historical context for evaluating metrics requires time and experience. Managers cannot expect comparison between how they did today and how they did yesterday to tell them something brilliant, however, comparing how they did today against the average performance over a month will provide them with some insightful thoughts.

While history takes time to develop, there is the more immediate context of outsider information. Here managers can always compare indicators against those of other organizations in similar situations through external benchmarking, a practice discussed in detail earlier. Two types of benchmarking are common. The first is where organizations compare themselves to the average performance of organizations in the industry. The second is where they compare themselves to industry leaders. The first kind of benchmarking is ideal in the early stages of the process as it gives organizations an indicator of where they need to be relative to rest of the industry. The latter is more suitable once they have gained more experience with the process and are looking to move up the charts and reach higher goals. An important point to bear in mind regarding benchmarking is that organizations must compare themselves to one that is comparable in terms of operations – apples with apples and oranges with oranges. Unless there is some base for commonality, comparing two organizations will not be grounded in any reality, resulting in discovery of information that is not valid or useful.

The fourth step involves devising appropriate interventions to improve the performance of certain areas. Interventions can serve as positive or negative reinforcements. Positive reinforcements involve understanding what worked well and continuing to do it in order to make the process stronger. Negative reinforcements entail uncovering what went wrong, correcting it and then ensuring that the correction is applied to improve the process. For example, if you know that your vendor selection process is satisfactory and sound, you must make sure that all successive projects follow the stated methodology so as to gain the same positive results. On the other hand, if you uncover short-comings in your attempts to transition the project, these must be identified and suitable alternatives should be devised and implemented. Managing knowledge, as discussed in the previous section, helps in devising appropriate interventions. The fourth step feeds back into the second or third step, depending on whether you need to calibrate new measures. If new measures are required, you go back to the second step, otherwise to the third step.

Measuring outputs

Output measures are derived from an understanding of what the customer of the process wants. In the case of outsourcing, organizations can have internal and external customers. If they outsource human resource functions such as payroll processing and employee benefits administration, the customers of interest are their employees. If organizations outsource the management of a call center, the customers of their products and service who call the center are the customers they are interested in.

Not surprisingly, the first step in developing good output measures is the identification of customers and their needs. Organizations normally have multiple categories of customers to a process. While all customers may share certain characteristics, there may be differences in the experiences and needs that can be used to segment them (Desouza and Awazu, 2005b). Experienced customers will have different needs from new ones; similarly, the needs of frequent or repeat customers will vary from those of occasional customers. It is always a good idea to get inputs on what is important from all segments of customers, as doing so will give organizations a better grasp of the complete picture.

The second step involves devising surveys or other instruments to get customer perceptions on the phenomena. Here the overriding rule is the KISS principle – Keep it simple, stupid! Nothing will detract customers from providing input faster than a long and cumbersome survey to fill in. Customers must be polled routinely and frequently for their opinions, yet they must not feel imposed upon. Sounds contradictory? Well, it is not. Customers can be routinely polled as they interact with an outsourced product or service, through surveys containing questions that can be answered with minimum intrusion on their time. Organizations must remember that customers are the ones who interact with the artifact being outsourced and their opinions should matter and must be accounted for. Customers will get frustrated – and very quickly, one might add! – if they see their opinions being ignored and failing to make a difference in how the product or service is being delivered. The third and fourth steps of measuring outputs are the same as for process metrics and hence need not be repeated here.

Points to bear in mind regarding metrics

1. Measure a stable process
2. Understand the nature of and variations in processes
3. Use multiple measures
4. Never manipulate metrics

Points to bear in mind regarding metrics

Metrics are one of the most abused and misused tools in the management arsenal. Think about Enron and the issues surrounding the auditing of their financial health. In the final analysis, financial statements represent metrics about a company's performance; they are the acid test against which the market makes a judgment on the company's future. In the context of outsourcing, metrics can also be misused – many a time this is because managers fail to recognize and appreciate the true qualities of metrics. Here are some points to bear in mind.

First, metrics are meaningful only if organizations have a stable process in place. Measuring unstable or chaotic processes will result in unstable and chaotic measures – measures that they cannot compare against or use with any clarity. It is essential that managers have a stable process in place before they go about the business of measurement. Consider what might happen if every time someone goes to measure an athlete's time to complete a 100-meter race he or she changed the definition of '100 meters'. Similarly, consider what might happen if organizations continuously changed the output when measuring customer satisfaction. The customer would be at a loss in terms of what to compare the current output against. To this end, it is important that managers recognize the need to establish a well-articulated and defined outsourcing program. Organizations must have a defined process that produces a defined output. Once the basic process is in place they can start to gather meaningful metrics about the process. The process and output can be improved and they will be able to use metrics in a meaningful way.

Second, organizations must understand the nature of processes and variations in processes. Variations are the major component of any approach to process control. Simply put, variations are deviations from the expected. Let us say that you expect a process to take, on average,

3 days to complete and you finish it in 2; you have a variance of −1. Similarly, if you finish it in 4 days you have a variance of +1. Variations or variability is normally of two kinds: natural or system variation and special-cause variation. The former is the kind of variance you expect because of the very nature of the process. With every repetition of the process, while the average time taken might be 3 days, you could expect it to be anywhere between 2 and 4 days. Natural variations are expected and must not be the focus of a great deal of management scrutiny since they *do* happen and are a normal part of operations. Special-cause variations are deviations from the expected caused by some problems or exceptions. For example, consider the case of a basketball player who is accustomed to scoring 20 points a game on average. One would expect the scores for a good and steady game to be within a range, the natural variation, where sometimes the player might score up to 30 points and at other times may score as low as 8 or 9. Thus, over a series of games the average stays intact. However, if the player scores no points during a game, or pours in 50 points another night, these are not natural occurrences and warrant his coach's attention. For any process, it is therefore important to identify the expected measure of performance and define the range of accepted values, ie the minimum and maximum values in the range between which one expects most measurements to fall due to natural variations. When there are scores that fall outside the range one needs to pay serious attention. For example, if one manager repeatedly takes too long to complete vendor assessments in comparison to peer managers, the organization needs to find out why this is so. Alternatively, if a manager is very quick and successful in the task of vendor assessment the organizations also need to investigate why; maybe the manager has a special tactic or has learnt how to weed out unsuitable vendors through experience. This knowledge can be shared with others in the organization and can be codified into best practices that will, in turn, improve the performance of the rest of the managers.

Third, use of single indicators to measure a phenomenon is a dangerous proposition. Consider what would happen if organizations only used a individual's age as an indicator of his or her knowledge on a topic. In some fields, the older you are the less you know, due to the high rates of innovation. One's age will be a better indicator of one's knowledge if analyzed in the context of other work experiences, education and skill sets. Relying on one measure is also dangerous due to risks associated with measurement errors. Simply put, this method leaves no backup measure to fall back on should the one measure be incorrect. This is why when organizations store information on customers, they normally ask for information such as name, customer number and invoice number. Should one of these be wrong, they can use any of the others to retrieve customer information. Similarly, in outsourcing organizations must use a combination of measurements to gauge the performance of any stage or activity in the life cycle.

Finally, one must remember that where there is a will there is a way. If managers want to find ways to hide bad information and come up with deceptive scores on metrics, they can. Numbers can lie and it is often when numbers are made the focal point of personnel evaluation that the pressure is the greatest to massage them.

Outsourcing metrics should be used as tools for getting a sense of where things stand. They should be used somewhat like the dashboard of a car. Viewing the dashboard gives critical indicators of how the vehicle is performing. If there are problems, for example if the engine is overheating, this information can be brought to the driver's attention for further inspection. Imagine what would happen if someone manipulated the mileage of the car. By doing that, maybe he or she can fool others into believing that the car is less used than it actually is, but what about fooling the driver of the vehicle? Manipulating the mileage may in fact result in the driver paying less attention to the various car maintenance activities needed, such as services and oil changes. In the end, manipulation of indicators does not help organizations get a true sense of their environment and will only come back to haunt them.

Outsourcing Management Maturity Model (OMMM)

Knowledge management and devising adequate metrics are signs of a mature outsourcing process. Consequently, when these are not in place organizations have an immature and incomplete outsourcing program. In this section, we will integrate the concepts of knowledge management and metrics to chart out an Outsourcing Management Maturity Model (OMMM).

Organizations engaging in outsourcing initiatives differ in their maturity and the consequent sophistication and success with which these engagements are executed. Maturity encompasses more than its common connotation of age or experience. It is common to assume that as we get older we become wiser and with experience we may be more sophisticated in our approach to solving problems. While this may be true for the most part, we all know of exceptions. We can find adults who throw tantrums and youngsters who display high levels of maturity. We can attribute this to proper management of oneself. The quicker we learn from our mistakes and change the underlying behavior causing the mistakes, the better we are positioned to be successful in the future.

Maturity models are common in all fields, ranging from education, quality management and software engineering, to sociology. Maslow was among the first scholars to construct a maturity model when he elaborated on the hierarchy of human needs. The most famous maturity model was developed by the Software Engineering Institute at Carnegie Mellon University for the purpose of streamlining the management of software projects – the Capability Maturity Model (CMM) (Humphrey, 1993; Paulk, Curtis and Chrissis, 1991; Saiedian and Kuzara, 1995). CMM has been refined, adapted and implemented by a number of organizations to help them manage their software projects.

CMM consists of a five-level maturity scale ranging from ad-hoc or chaotic software processes to optimized and well-executed software management functions. The levels are arranged in such a manner that capacity at the lower levels forms a strong foundation from which an organization can move to the upper levels. The various levels represent initial, repeatable, defined, managed and optimized phases of software process management. At the initial level, an organization is characterized as functioning with ad-hoc and chaotic processes. In most cases, no formal procedures and project plans are in place and if present, they lack any implementation mechanisms. At the repeatable level, the organization has basic project controls in place, ie project management, product assurance and change control. Here, the organization demonstrates how to conduct repeatable processes efficiently and effectively although it has a tendency to struggle when faced with new problems. At the defined level, the organization has established a foundation for the examination of processes and devised some initial approaches to improve the processes. At the managed level, the organization establishes quality and productivity measurements. At the optimized level, the organization's efforts are solely focused on identifying weak elements and strengthening the process by removing deficiencies.

The CMM model has become the benchmark for evaluating software processes in organizations. It is used for evaluating organizations when bids are solicited on software engineering projects and also as a benchmarking tool to aid in process improvement. Movement up and through the CMM model requires becoming better at all aspects of the software process. Using the CMM framework, it is possible to devise an OMMM. Based on our experience, we can argue that much of the needs and rationale that led to the creation of the CMM are evident in the outsourcing world and hence require an OMMM (see Figure 10.1). The various stages of this model are described below.

Stage 1 is dominated by a chaotic and ad-hoc process. The organization will lack a thorough understanding of what comprises the entire life cycle of outsourcing and will not know any one part of the process in any detail. Moreover, the manner in which the various stages of outsourcing are conducted will resemble an ad-hoc and incomplete process. The organization will witness minimal or no benefits in using outsourcing as a strategic tool.

At Stage 2, the organization starts to become reactive by improving various parts of the outsourcing process owing to external pressures.

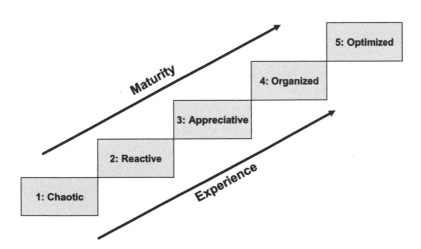

Figure 10.1 Outsourcing Management Maturity Model (OMMM)

For instance, the organization may expend energies to improve the process of vendor assessment or contract management. As pressures are applied on parts of the outsourcing process, these areas increase in sophistication and maturity. While these areas improve their performance, the other stages will not improve at the same pace. Moreover, the connections between the stages of the outsourcing life cycle will also be poor. The adage, 'You are only as strong as your weakest link' holds true here. The overall outsourcing life cycle will have minimal improvement over the ad-hoc stage, though a select few stages of the process will be significantly improved.

At Stage 3, the organization has assembled a basic, yet fragile, outsourcing program. The various stages of outsourcing are connected and linked, thus allowing for a truly process-centric view of outsourcing. By connecting the various stages of the outsourcing process managers have a better sense of how each stage affects the succeeding one. Metrics begin to emerge at this stage as managers can now conceptualize the outsourcing process, though many of the metrics will be basic and rudimentary.

At Stage 4, the organization has an organized and well-defined process in place and will begin to reap the benefits of this sound outsourcing program. The outsourcing methodology is applied in a unified fashion. More complex forms of metrics can be developed here as organizations have a better definition of the outsourcing process, which is a stable one. We see the emergence of departments that are responsible for managing the outsourcing process. Knowledge of best practices in conducting outsourcing will also start to get documented. Lotus Corporation created what it calls its '35 rules of thumb' to manage each phase of an alliance, from formation to termination (Dyer, Kale and Singh, 2001). Hewlett-Packard developed 60 different tools and templates, included in a 300-page manual to guide decision making in specific alliance situations (Dyer, Kale and Singh, 2001). The manual included such tools as a template for making the business case for an alliance, a partner-evaluation form, a negotiations template outlining the roles and responsibilities of different departments, a list of ways to measure alliance performance and an alliance-termination checklist. Eli Lilly created an office of alliance management (OAM) that facilitates the development and implementation of best practices throughout the company. Alliance management in the OAM is responsible for capturing and codifying knowledge about the management of their alliances for future references (Dyer, Kale and Singh, 2001).

The focus of Stage 5 will be on improving the outsourcing methodology. Knowledge-management activities will begin to reap value here, as new experiences and insights begin to contribute to the improvement of the process. As noted in the section on metrics, both positive and negative reinforcements will be used to improve the outsourcing process. Unless an organization keeps its outsourcing process up to date and continuously seeks ways to improve it, it will slip back to Stage 4. This backslide is analogous to when an athlete stops practicing – painstakingly built-up muscles will begin to slacken into fat and agility in movement will be replaced by sluggishness. Constant updating and reinforcement is critical to sustaining a Stage 5 maturity.

To summarize, an organization moving through the outsourcing maturity stages must attend to several matters. First, it is important for the organization to work out and put in place a well-defined outsourcing process. This will only occur with time and with experience. During the early stages things will be chaotic, and expectedly so. The organization must realize that this is only temporary and can be remedied if it works consistently at putting a well-defined outsourcing process in place. Once a process is in place, the next step is to begin refining and improving it. This will call for two activities – knowledge management and development of metrics. Knowledge management will help by capturing experiences, both good and bad, that take place when engaging in outsourcing and these experiences can then be organized and synthesized to work out enhancements and improvements. Metrics are important to continuously improve the process by having something to measure the state of the process and compare it against.

Relationship management office (RMO)

Outsourcing, like all other serious business matters such as finance, marketing or human resources, needs to be housed within a department in the organization. This department must be responsible for overseeing all efforts in the context of outsourcing at an operational, tactical and strategic level. The senior manager of this department must be able to connect with other senior managers in the various domains and present outsourcing issues at the strategic levels of the organization.

Mature organizations will have a relationship management office (RMO) in place to oversee outsourcing efforts and manage the portfolio of existing outsourcing arrangements. Managing knowledge effectively is central to achieving these outcomes. Most RMOs are chartered to:

- ensure that there is consistency in terms of outsourcing objectives and business objectives;
- conduct feasibility analyses of outsourcing projects at a global level and look at issues of opportunity cost of resources;
- coordinate efforts among managers and their assignments to ensure that the right hand knows what the left is doing, instead of washing away what the left is doing, and ensure that outsourcing efforts are managed effectively;
- conduct reviews and assessments such as postmortem analyses, develop lessons learnt and manage a knowledge base to be used for informing future efforts;
- serve as an information integrator – ie the RMO can be viewed as a dashboard that has the vital information on outsourcing projects under way at the organization;
- ensure adherence to standardized outsourcing methodologies and processes so as to have a unified working framework;
- evaluate the portfolio of outsourcing endeavors on a routine basis to calculate their business value, avoid redundancies in effort, manage risks and manage metrics.

Setting up an RMO is only beneficial if this unit is allowed to succeed and deliver results. Successful RMOs have very clear reporting lines identified. Roles, responsibilities and accountability issues are clearly identified, defined and implemented. To be successful, an RMO must also have the necessary resources to accomplish scheduled tasks. Different options include:

- Having the RMO as an independent group.
- Creating an RMO to report to an executive within a functional department. This option may be good for organizations that work on multiple yet independent assignments; for example, if a company manufacturers PCs and is also in the automobile business, it can have two RMOs to undertake activities within each area.

● Creating RMOs based on geographical locations to oversee local projects. In this case there will be a need to establish chains of control and accountability protocols to handle work involving multiple global sites. Most RMOs need to have only a small group of dedicated staff personnel to oversee the daily operations. However, they must be able to have access to staff in the various functional sectors so as to draw on them as needed by the various outsourcing projects.

RMOs in different organizations differ in their scope and roles. Research on project management offices (Desouza and Awazu, 2005c) indicates that there are four major classes of RMO. At the most basic level, the RMO will be an information integrator. Here the RMO just stores information that is needed to manage the overall work of the organization. RMOs as information integrator are common in organizations that are just getting started with outsourcing. These RMOs basically serve as distributors of information so that management can adequately move through the various stages of the outsourcing life cycle.

At the second level, in addition to being an information integrator, the RMO will also serve as an evaluator ensuring that standardized tools and processes are being used and will be responsible for coordination of metrics. RMOs who serve as evaluators are normally a step-up from the information integrators. Here, the RMO has established a common methodology for conducting outsourcing and now wants to make sure that everyone in the organization follows the established guidelines and processes so as to get the maximum results.

At the third level, in addition to being an information integrator and an evaluator ensuring that standardized tools and processes are being implemented, the RMO will be a synchronizer of tasks and projects ensuring coordination among outsourcing projects and also being a house of best practices. The job of this RMO is to serve as passive coach for the managers by informing them about best practices and how to improve their performance. The goal of the RMO at this level will be to help the organization move from having an organized outsourcing process to one that is continuously being improved by the sharing and application of new knowledge.

At the fourth level, the RMO will be a separate business unit responsible for coordination across the sectors of the organization, setting goals and spanning multiple projects. Here the RMO has the highest level of authority and serves as the manager of project managers. Moreover, rather than being a passive coach for improving the outsourcing practice in the organization, the RMO will take an active role in ensuring that knowledge is disseminated to the project managers and that such knowledge is applied.

Conclusion

This chapter has discussed how best to improve the process of outsourcing by paying attention to the concepts of knowledge management, metrics, the OMMM and the RMO. Improving the process of outsourcing is not a costless or easy feat to accomplish. Management must be willing to 'put their money where their mouth is', so to speak. As discussed in the section on knowledge management, learning initiatives take time, effort and failures before they materialize. Managers who expect to get it right the first time and those who are not ready to bear the initial cost of learning will have failed outsourcing programs. Failures should be examined openly and frankly within the organization, more as a source for learning and getting at the root cause of problems than to become a blame game.

The task of managing metrics is equally challenging. Numbers will lie if you want them to. Most managers put a lot of weight into 'making numbers', but doing this will call for hiding or not disclosing negative information and may lead to serious repercussions. Organizations must realize that metrics are just that – measurements or indicators. They should not be used to jump to conclusions without thorough investigation. Moreover, metrics are only of value if they are used as a means for challenging the organization to do its best and improve performance. Conversely, they can be harmful if people devise ways to work around the metrics and provide meaningless information. Developing valid and reliable metrics takes time and effort. We have depicted a maturity trajectory that organizations normally follow in order to improve their processes. The critical point to remember is that no organization can jump interventions needed to move through the various stages of maturity. For instance, it will not be possible to think in terms of optimizing the outsourcing process without first having a process that is stable and non-chaotic. Finally, decision rights regarding outsourcing need to be centralized and coordinated within a unit of the organization. We have called the unit an RMO. The exact nature and type of the RMO will depend on how much accountability, authority and responsibility is vested in the unit, and the scope of its operations.

In the final chapter we survey the best practices found in organizations that have mastered the outsourcing process. Then, we pull out our crystal ball and hypothesize about what the future might hold for outsourcing.

11 Industry best practices

In the preceding chapters we have walked through the various stages of the outsourcing life cycle, providing you with pointers of things to beware of and things to do in order to accomplish your goals successfully. In this final chapter, we will recap the crucial points to bear in mind when engaging in an outsourcing initiative – the best practices. In conclusion, we will tell you how we expect outsourcing practices to change over the next few years.

Best practices in outsourcing

1. Outsource for business value and strategic advantages
2. Specify your needs – do not have it done for you
3. Shop around for a vendor using multiple criteria
4. Ensure negotiation and contracting for a win-win situation
5. Do not be rigid during project initiation and transition
6. Have well-defined metrics
7. Always have a viable exit strategy
8. Do not be content with the process – improve continuously

Best practices

The best practices outlined here have been deduced from our study of a number of outsourcing engagements and also by actively participating in many engagements. Rather than being specific in terms of naming organizations that have put these practices in place, we will opt to present the practices in general. This will help us avoid issues such as showing favoritism or endorsing any one organization. After all, an organization may be good at one thing in one context and may have hopelessly inadequate practices in another context.

1. Outsource for business value and strategic advantages

First, you need to be clear about the rationale for outsourcing. Do not outsource for meager operational issues or short-term benefits such as short-term and immediate cost benefits. In this situation, the cost of carrying out the outsourcing endeavor will far outweigh any benefits you plan on receiving. As discussed in Chapter 3, make sure that you have exercised due diligence in conducting your strategic assessment. When outsourcing, it is absolutely critical to ensure that the outsourcing project is in keeping with the current strategic position of your organization and with its future directions. It is equally important to ensure that when they outsource, organizations are contributing to their business value and also increasing strategic advantages. Anything short of this will lead them to conduct a rather expensive outsourcing endeavor with few, if any, long-term lasting benefits. It is also critical to get senior-level executive sponsorship for the outsourcing effort. Senior executives have the ability to rally support behind the effort, which is a critical ingredient for success. If your organization's senior executives are not convinced about the business value of the outsourcing effort, or if they think the project is not important enough for them to get involved in, they will not actively take part in the effort and this negative signal will doom the outsourcing effort from the onset.

2. Specify your needs – do not have it done for you

It must be clear who is outsourcing to whom. *You* must be in charge of defining the needs and goals of the outsourcing project. Too often, companies fail to realize the importance of taking the first steps and spending the due resources needed to clearly specify their needs up front (see Chapter 4). Failure to specify your organization's needs properly results in an incomplete and poor negotiation session with the vendor. This is where the vendor organization has the greatest potential to leverage its own position, by being 'helpful' and *specifying your requirements for you*. The chances are high that vendors will specify things that they can do and do well, and will avoid paying attention to areas where they lack competency – after all they want your business. In the end, you will get a product or service out of the outsourcing relationship that you happened to agree to, but never really needed! We cannot overstate how important it is to conduct a thorough needs analysis *independent* of the vendor to get a true sense of your own needs.

3. Shop around for a vendor using multiple criteria

Do not ever shop around for a vendor using just a single criterion. Most often, this criterion is cost. As illogical as this may seem, most organizations first pre-screen vendors based on cost (see Chapter 5). Vendors will always 'low-ball' (present low costs) in the beginning – this is because they know that organizations will pre-screen incoming bids based on costs. A vendor who offers a lower price than everyone else may be very good at what it does, but the chances of this are low – unless you are hearing from an industry leader with an established reputation. Most of the time vendors who low-ball on price are usually desperate for new business and will say anything to get a signed contract. After you have signed on that dotted line, you will pay more in terms of receiving a lower quality product or service. Vendors *must* be evaluated on multiple criteria such as quality, reputation and experiences, with cost as the last factor.

4. Negotiate and contract for a win-win situation

Remember that you are entering into a relationship with a business partner. The chances of the success of this relationship are higher when both parties are in a win-win situation. This is the same rule that we follow in formalizing personal relationships. When negotiating and developing a contract (see Chapter 6) you must not get too selfish and try to squeeze maximal returns from the vendor, as any such gains will only be on paper and not during the lifetime of the relationship. A vendor is your business partner and must want to sustain the relationship just as much as you do, because it is winning from the relationship as well.

5. Do not be rigid during project initiation and transition

As outlined in Chapter 7, the initial stages of outsourcing are fraught with chaotic and confusing behavior. Experienced outsourcing practitioners know that this is to be expected and part of the business. It is the inexperienced managers who panic and get overly concerned and become rigid in their handling of the situation, constantly seeking answers for problems by referring to the contract. Flexibility is the predominant characteristic required to get through the initial stages of the outsourcing work. Managers must recognize that this is a stage where two organizations that have never interacted before are joining forces. Areas of friction must be accepted and used positively to build a budding future relationship.

6. Have well-defined metrics

Measurement is important and often overlooked by novices in outsourcing. It is essential to have well-defined and agreed metrics to evaluate the state of the outsourcing relationship (see Chapter 10). Metrics take the guesswork out of the outsourcing engagement and give critical indicators against which to benchmark performance. Metrics need to be simple, concrete and comprehensive and must account for the process and output aspects of the outsourcing efforts.

7. Always have a viable exit strategy

Plan ahead by assuming that there will be problems and you may have to exit the relationship urgently, with possible hostility involved (see Chapter 9). It is crucial to have an exit strategy from the very onset when getting into an outsourcing relationship. After all, you cannot control the future of your vendor or business partner. Unusual circumstances may result in the vendor not being able to perform its tasks or in your no longer wanting to continue the relationship. In situations like these, you must have a backup plan that can be activated. Do not make the mistake of assuming that your vendor is thoughtful and has a backup strategy in place to attend to your needs. If you are lucky and have such a vendor, great! But, chances are high that this will not be the case. The vendor will be too busy dealing with its own crisis to care about your needs. The bottom line is *do not start an outsourcing relationship without having an exit strategy handy*.

8. Do not be content with the process – improve continuously

Improvement of the outsourcing process must be a continuous quest. Any process can be improved or built upon. It will be unwise to claim than an outsourcing process has reached its optimal level. You may have a very good outsourcing process in place, but there are always things that can be done better. It is through embracing these improvements that you will improve the overall process. It is our belief that an organization's outsourcing capability is going to be a strategic differentiator. This is where how good your process is compared to others in your industries makes a difference. You must be ready to be the best and work towards it. Having a stagnant outsourcing process will not serve strategic purposes.

The future of outsourcing

The future of outsourcing is bright. There are several things that will occur in the immediate future. First, the backlash and emotional stances regarding the outsourcing of knowledge work will come to an end, because of the simple reality that the economics of outsourcing outweigh these concerns significantly. Second, the transformation of outsourcing knowledge work, such as software development and R&D activities, will increase and become more accepted. This will pave the way for organizations to become more comfortable outsourcing more complex matters and matters of greater significance, such as core competencies. Third, the outsourcing decision, which is currently dominated by cost considerations will shift to one of knowledge considerations – ie who the expert in a domain is, rather than who is the lowest cost provider. Finally, there will be leaders and laggards in any given industry, based on how effective their outsourcing programs are. This is bound to happen as more organizations become decentralized and based on variable-cost rather than fixed-cost models to meet the characteristics of a dynamic marketplace. As for the distant future, we do not want to postulate anything, as we would still have to get out a crystal ball!

Final comments

It has been our pleasure to share with you our thoughts on and experiences in outsourcing. We hope that you have enjoyed the book. Please do send us comments about its content to enhance our knowledge and views on outsourcing. Moreover, we hope that this book helps you to be more successful in using outsourcing as a strategic weapon for enhancing your organization's current competitive position and also in helping you transform your business to be better prepared for the future.

References

Davenport, T H and Prusak, L (1998) *Working Knowledge: How organizations manage what they know*, Harvard Business School Press, Boston, MA

Desouza, K C and Awazu, Y (2005a) *Engaged Knowledge Management: Engagement with new realities*, Palgrave Macmillan, Basingstoke

Desouza, K C and Awazu, Y (2005b) What do they know?, *Business Strategy Review*, **16** (1), pp 41–45

Desouza, K C and Awazu, Y (2005c) Project management offices in software organizations, Working Paper, Institute for Engaged Business Research, The Engaged Enterprise

Desouza, K C and Evaristo, J R (2005) Managing knowledge in distributed projects, *Communications of the ACM*, **47** (4), pp 87–91

Desouza, K C and Vanapalli, G K (2005) Securing knowledge in organizations: Lessons from the defense and intelligence sectors, *International Journal of Information Management*, **25** (1), pp 85–98

Desouza, K C, Dingsøyr, T and Awazu, Y (2005) Experiences with conducting project postmortems: Reports vs. stories, *Software Process Improvement and Practice*, **10**, (2), pp 203–15

Dyer, J H, Kale, P and Singh, H (2001) How to make strategic alliances work, *Sloan Management Review*, **42** (4), pp 37–43

Field, T (2001a) Homegrown talent, *CIO Magazine*, 1 October 2001

Field, T (2001b) Outsourced in America, *CIO Magazine*, 1 October 2001

Humphrey, W S (1993) *Introduction to software process improvement*, Software Engineering Institute, Carnegie Melon University, Pittsburgh, PA

McDougall, P (2004a) Aon outsourcing IT for savings and enhanced security, *InformationWeek*, 25 May 2004

McDougall, P (2004b) Aon signs $600 million outsourcing deal with CSC, *InformationWeek*, 25 May 2004

Nonaka, I and Takeuchi H (1995) *The Knowledge-creating company: How Japanese companies create the dynamics of innovation*, Oxford University Press, New York

Patton, S (2005) A new way to manage vendors, *CIO Magazine*, 1 February, 2005

Paulk, M C, Curtis, B and Chrissis, M B (1991) *Capability maturity model for software*, Software Engineering Institute, Carnegie Melon University, Pittsburgh

Power, M, Desouza, K C and Bonifazi, C (2005) Developing superior outsourcing programs, *IEEE IT Professional*, July/August

Power, M, Bonifazi, C and Desouza, K C (2004) Ten outsourcing traps to avoid, *Journal of Business Strategy*, **25** (2), pp 37–42

Saiedian, H and Kuzara, R (1995) SEI capability maturity model's impact on contractors, *IEEE Software*, **28** (1), pp 16–26

Index

NB: page numbers in *italic* indicate figures or tables

Also available from Kogan Page

Advanced Project Management, 2004, Alan Orr

Bids, Tenders & Proposals: Winning business through best practice, 2nd edn, 2005, Harold Lewis

Bridging the Culture Gap: A practical guide to international business communication, 2004, Penny Carté and Chris Fox

Building Tomorrow's Company: A guide to sustainable business success, 2002, Philip Sadler

The Business Plan Workbook, 5th edn, 2005, Colin Barrow, Paul Barrow and Robert Brown

Business Solutions on Demand: Creating customer value at the speed of light, 2004, Mark Cerasale and Merlin Stone

Change Management Excellence: Using the four intelligences for successful organizational change, 2004, Sarah Cook, Steve Macaulay and Hilary Coldicott

The Company Secretary's Handbook: A guide to duties and responsibilities, 3rd edn, 2004, Helen Ashton

Consultant – Market Yourself: Raise your profile and attract new business, 2002, Robert Gentle

Consultants & Advisers: A best practice guide to choosing, using and getting good value, 2004, Harold Lewis

The Corporate Finance Handbook, 4th edn, 2006, Jonathan Reuvid

Creative Business Presentations: Inventive ideas for making an instant impact, 2003, Eleri Sampson

Cross-cultural Communication: The essential guide to international management, 2003, John Mattock

The 18 Immutable Laws of Corporate Reputation: Creating, protecting and repairing your most valuable asset, 2004, Ron Alsop

The Employer's Handbook: An essential guide to employment law, personnel policies and procedures, 3rd edn, 2005, Barry Cushway

Financial Management for the Small Business, 6th edn, 2006, Colin Barrow

Goal Directed Project Management, 3rd edn, 2004, Coopers & Lybrand

Going Public: The Essential Guide to Flotation, 2nd edn, 2006, Jonathan Reuvid

Growing a Private Company: Commercial strategies for building a business worth millions, 2000, Ian Smith

A Handbook of Management and Leadership: A guide to managing for results, 2005, Michael Armstrong and Tina Stephens

A Handbook of Management Techniques: The best selling guide to modern management methods, 3rd edn, 2001, Michael Armstrong

The Handbook of Personal Wealth Management: How to ensure maximum return and security, 2005, Jonathan Reuvid

The Handbook of Project Management: A practical guide to effective policies and procedures, 2nd edn, 2003, Trevor L Young

Hard-core Management: What you wont learn from the business gurus, 2003, Jo Owen

Having Their Cake: How the city and big bosses are consuming UK business, 2004, Don Young and Pat Scott

The Health and Safety Handbook: A practical guide to health and safety law, management policies and procedures, 2006, Jeremy Stranks

The Healthy Organization: A revolutionary approach to people and management, 2nd edn, 2004, Brian Dive

How to Be an Even Better Manager: A complete A to Z of proven techniques and essential skills, 6th edn, 2004, Michael Armstrong

How to Grow Leaders: The seven key principles of effective leadership development, 2005, John Adair

How to Invest in Hedge Funds: An investment professional's guide, 2004, Matt Ridley

How to Understand the Financial Pages: A guide to money and the jargon, 2005, Alexander Davidson

The Inspirational Leader: How to motivate, encourage and achieve success, 2005, John Adair

IT Governance: A manager's guide to data security and BS 7799 / ISO 17799, 3rd edn, 2005, Alan Calder and Steve Watkins

Making Sense of Change Management: A complete guide to the models, tools and techniques of organizational change, 2004, Esther Cameron and Mike Green

Management Consultancy in Practice: Award-winning international case studies, 2004, Fiona Czerniawska and Paul May

Management Stripped Bare: What they don't teach you at business school, 2002, Jo Owen

Managing Business Risk: A practical guide to protecting your business, 3rd edn, 2006, Jonathan Reuvid

Managing People in a Small Business, 2002, John Stredwick

Marketing Communications: An integrated approach, 4th edn, 2004, P R Smith and Jonathan Taylor

Not Bosses But Leaders: How to lead the way to success, 3rd edn, 2002, John Adair

The Practice of Project Management: A guide to the business-focussed approach, 2002, Dennis Comninos and Enzo Frigenti

Project Risk Management: An essential tool for managing and controlling projects, 2004, D van Well-Stam, F Lindenaar, S van Kinderen and BP van den Bunt

Raising Finance: A practical guide for starting, expanding and selling your business, 2004, Paul Barrow

Strategic Business Planning: A dynamic system for improving performance and competitive advantage, 2nd edn, 2004, Clive Reading

Strategic Planning Workbook, 2002, Neville Lake

The Sustainable Enterprise: Profiting from best practice, 2005, Christopher Brown

The Top Consultant: Developing your skills for greater effectiveness, 4th edn, 2004, Calvert Markham

Venture Capital Funding: A practical guide to raising finance, 2005, Stephen Bloomfield

The above titles are available from all good bookshops or direct from the publishers. To obtain more information, please contact the publisher at the address below:

Kogan Page
120 Pentonville Road
London N1 9JN
Tel: 020 7278 0433
Fax: 020 7837 6348
www.kogan-page.co.uk

BASEMENT

JAN. 2010